The Journey

RESPONDING SKILLFULLY TO THE CIRCUMSTANCES OF LIFE

DON GRIFFIN

WESTBOW
PRESS
A DIVISION OF THOMAS NELSON

WestBow Press books may be ordered through booksellers or by contacting:

WestBow Press
A Division of Thomas Nelson
1663 Liberty Drive
Bloomington, IN 47403
www.westbowpress.com
1-(866) 928-1240

ISBN: 978-1-4497-8940-4 (sc)
ISBN: 978-1-4497-8941-1 (hc)
ISBN: 978-1-4497-8939-8 (e)

Library of Congress Control Number: 2013905340

Printed in the United States of America.

WestBow Press rev. date: 4/2/2013

TABLE OF CONTENTS

INTRODUCTION

The Christian life can be the most joy-filled life possible because it comes from the hand of a benevolent and loving God who, according to 1 Timothy 6:17, is gracious enough to give us a life that can be filled with excitement and anticipation as He guides us in the great adventure of knowing and serving Him.

Yes, God does give us everything for our enjoyment. What can be compared to the birth of a new child? When your children make godly choices and stand for what is right, how could you be any more proud of them? What could possibly describe the fulfillment that comes from having met the person who will be your companion throughout life? Who can describe the intense joy that believers many times feel as they worship together in church with their brothers and sisters? What a wonderful and blessed thing it is to have fellow church members who are like family.

Many are the joys of those who know and love the Lord. They are the most blessed people on the earth. God's great favor toward us causes us to join with the psalm writer in Psalm 48:1 in exclaiming, "Great is the LORD, and most worthy of praise." Truly there is nothing like living a life that has meaning and purpose, and that will last throughout eternity.

On the other hand, it also must be recognized that although the Christian life is joyful, it is often times not comfortable. Anyone who thinks it is easy to live a holy, God-honoring life in our sinful world knows little about being a disciple of Christ. As we continue our pilgrimage in this world, we can expect explosive land mines to be planted around us, dangerous storms to threaten us, and unfair circumstances to sometimes overwhelm us. That is the bad news.

The good news is the fact that God promises to always be our Helper and Guide. He gives strength when we are weak and wisdom when we need direction. As we learn His Word and live by His principles, we become skillful in living in a world that stumbles in ignorance and spiritual darkness.

A large part of living as an "overcomer" rather than a victim is understanding the greatness of God. If we recognize Him for who He is and walk in His ways, we will be able to be confident in the battle. The apostle John said in 1 John 4:4, "You, dear children, are from God and have overcome them, because the one who is in you is greater than the one who is in the world."

The message of the entire Bible shouts the praise of the Almighty, and meditating on who He is should leave us stunned in amazement. To think that He spoke the worlds into existence and now sustains everything by His mighty power is totally beyond my wildest imagination. To think that the fullness of His being is everywhere at the same time is a concept that leaves me speechless. He is the eternal Spirit who transcends everything, anywhere. At the same time, He is my Father and promises to always be with me.

He lives outside what we call time, but He is aware of all my days. He knew when I would be born, and He knows when I will die. Although He is perfectly holy and pure, He wants to forgive my sins and have fellowship with me.

What we call "outer space" defies our greatest scientific discoveries and makes all of our accumulated knowledge seem insignificant by comparison, and yet He made it all and fills it all. Although He fills the indescribable immensity of outer space, He has a perfect understanding of our personal lives. He cares enough to bend down to comfort our broken hearts and to be our own Counselor and Guide.

The psalm writer illustrated the omniscience of God when he said in Psalm 139:4, "Before a word is on my tongue you know it completely, O LORD." God not only knows what we say, He also knows what we are going to say before we speak the words. This Almighty God is aware of everything about us. He knows our strengths and weaknesses, our fears and dreams. Doubtless the apostle Paul was awestricken when he contemplated the nature, the majesty, and the power of God. Paul expressed his thoughts about the Lord well in Romans 11:34-36:

> Oh, the depth of the riches of the wisdom and knowledge of God!
>> How unsearchable his judgments,
>> and his paths beyond tracing out!
> "Who has known the mind of the Lord?
>> Or who has been his counselor?"
> "Who has ever given to God,
>> that God should repay him?"
> For from him and through him and to him are all things.
>> To him be the glory forever! Amen.

Through a series of devotional readings, *The Journey* urges us to be fully devoted to God. It instructs us to trust in Him with all of our hearts even when He doesn't seem to be concerned about the seemingly negative circumstances in our lives. The book reminds us of the fact that God always has a reason for the things He allows in our lives. As we walk through deep waters, it is our duty to honor Him through faith, holiness, and an unwillingness to compromise.

These devotionals are not deeply theological. They are practical lessons that are easily understood and identified with by the reader. Some are based on my life and the lives of my family members. Others find their source in everyday life situations that we all experience. Some will make you laugh, while others may make you cry.

My prayer is that you will experience a sense of adoration and worship to God woven through the pages of the book so that you will end each chapter hungering to have a deeper walk with the Master.

CHAPTER 1

THE GRAB BAG OF LIFE

Every person walks through the journey of life without knowing what the future holds for him or her. The most carefully laid plans guarantee nothing. What we do know is that all of us will experience some good and some bad. In every life, there will be times of laughter and times of crying. We are all well acquainted with the so-called ups and downs of life, and we never know whether today will be an "up" day or a "down" day.

To use an analogy, life is like a "grab bag." Have you ever gone into a baseball-card shop and purchased a grab bag? A grab bag is a bag containing merchandise that you cannot see. You buy it before you know what is in it. As you open your bag, you will probably find players of various skill and popularity. You may be delightfully surprised with a number of top-notch players, or you may feel that you have totally wasted your money on relatively unknown team members whom you don't care to have in your collection. Each card you pull out of the bag could make you very glad that you took a chance, or it could make you feel that you have made a poor investment.

Life, too, is a grab bag. Each day, you reach into the bag of life and pull out a card that outlines a series of events that you will experience on that particular day. Some days are just okay. Some are great, and others are days that you wish you could put back in the bag. However you may feel about a particular day, one thing is for sure: you are going to have to live with it.

We have no power to change which "cards" we receive in life. What we do have is the ability to choose how we respond to those cards. When God created mankind, He created us as thinking beings who are capable of making decisions. Unlike a robot that is programmed to respond in predetermined ways, we have the ability to reason logically and to be personally active in the events that impact our lives.

On the other hand, we need to be careful to not criticize someone who is struggling with discouragement, because you don't know what kind of cards he or she received. All of us have a unique blend of cards in our grab bags, so that no other person can completely understand another's happiness or pain. Consider what 1 Corinthians 2:11 says: "For who among men knows the thoughts of a man except the man's spirit within him? In the same way no one knows the thoughts of God except the Spirit of God."

If someone says, "I understand exactly how you feel," they don't. They can't. Proverbs 14:10 says, "Each heart knows its own bitterness, and no one else can share its joy." The psalm writer said no one understands completely how another person feels. Maybe that is best for all of us because a lot of our thoughts are far from being positive and edifying. If the truth were known, many times the smiles on our faces are not in our heart. The smiling face is only a mask that covers up the hurt that is on the inside.

The good news is that, apart from medical causes, no one has to live a depressed life. The cards you take out of your grab bag cannot force you to be miserable. It's a matter of choice. If you choose, you can be consumed by the bad cards that have been given to you, such as that problem person at work, a spouse who is hard to live with, or children who always seem to find trouble.

The Lord wants you to experience his joy even if your bag seems to be filled with cards you don't want. The book of Philippians is an illustration of this kind of joy because Paul wrote the book when he was suffering in prison—and yet his words are filled with rejoicing. The apostle Paul was in prison, but he was never alone. He spent his time in fellowship with the Savior and found joy in the midst of hardship: "Rejoice in the Lord always. I will say it again: Rejoice!" (Philippians 4:4). We have the same decision that Paul had. Do we mourn over the negative, or do we rejoice in the positive things God has done in our lives?

The Lord exhorts us to choose joy. Psalm 32:10-11 says, "Many are the woes of the wicked, but the LORD's unfailing love surrounds the man who trusts in him. Rejoice in the LORD and be glad, you righteous; sing, all you who are upright in heart!" Trust is the key, isn't it? It is trusting in God's unchanging goodness, His unlimited power, and His perfect wisdom that allows us to dispel worry and to rest in the power of Someone much greater than ourselves. That knowledge of God should give us joy, no matter how bad our cards seem to be. There is no circumstance in life that He is not greater than. Today you may have experienced a "bad card" day. As you pull another card out of the grab bag tomorrow, you may find it to be exactly what you need. So relax and rest in the arms of a father who constantly watches over you.

Lord, it is very hard to move away from selfishness and to believe in your faithfulness. Help us to do so, that we may experience your joy. Amen.

CHAPTER 2

THE JOY OF TODAY

Ask the average person when the best time of his life was. Although I cannot be sure of how he will answer you, I can be pretty sure of what he won't say. In all probability, he won't tell you that the best time of his life is his present experience. He is much more likely to point back to some previous time, sometimes when things were better, happier, and easier. One of the reasons for our love relationship with the past is the fact that we generally don't like change. More often than not, change is viewed as an enemy rather than a friend. It is this enemy that takes us out of our familiar rut and forces us into a lifestyle that requires us to adjust to a new way of living. Change threatens us with the unfamiliar, and we're not sure that we know how to deal with it.

Sometimes change becomes so elevated that it takes us into a new stage of life. Stages of life include such things as taking your child to school for the first day. The elementary years fly by, and then there is middle school. High school soon becomes a thing of the past, and your son or daughter is off to college—already? Like it or not, we all experience changes and stages of life. We go through them as we switch roles with our parents and become caregivers to those who once took care of us. We enter a new stage of life when, almost magically, some little child is calling you "grandmother" or "grandfather." And through all the frustration and weariness of soul and body that accompany changes, we sometimes find ourselves wishing for former days when things seemed simpler and less demanding. We are good at fantasizing about the past because we have the ability to practice selective remembering. We generally remember only what we choose to remember so that, in our blurred vision, we see the past as being something that it really never was. We forget that the "good old days" had their own share of stress, difficulties, failures, and frustrations.

From a biblical perspective, God tells us life consists of "seasons" that include both good and bad (see Ecclesiastes 3:1-8), and all of which are meant by our Creator to transform us so we become more holy, more Christ-like. What's more, each season is meant to prepare us for the next season until we reach the time when all of our seasons have ended, and then we will transition into a glorious eternity where all hurts and pain will be removed. All tears will be wiped away, and we will bask in the light of God's love throughout eternity (see Revelation 21:4).

Instead of longing, and sometimes even grieving, for that which will never again be, plant your feet down securely in the joy of present-day life, and learn to experience the sufficiency of God's grace for today. Part of making your current life a good memory in the future depends on the decisions you make now. If you seek God's will in your life and step into the work that He has already prepared for you, you will find yourself in a few years looking back on your present life with gratitude for the "good old days" of today.

So what part of your current life do you think you will soon be considering to be one of your best days? Whatever that thing is should not just be a future memory. It should be an encouragement to you. Tell yourself every day when you wake up, "I have the privilege of living with the blessing of God today. This is a time that I will one day consider blessed. When that time comes, I will wish I could live some of my present life over, but it will be too late. The good things about my life in my present circumstances can only be lived now."

On the other hand, a failure to do God's will today is a failure in life that will never go away. You will find His grace to be sufficient, and one day when all is said and done, you will realize His plan was perfect all along the way. He makes no mistakes.

Lord, help me to be content to live without wishing for the circumstances of yesterday. Help me to realize that I am building my future by the way I live today. In Jesus's name, I ask this. Amen.

Chapter 3

Playing the Game of Life

When I was much younger, I frequently visited my cousin when school was out. During the heat of those summer days when everything outside was melting or burning up, we would sit in the luxury of my grandmother's cool, air-conditioned living room and play board games. Being the great host that she was, my grandmother would serve us large glasses of Coca-Cola with ice cream in them and would periodically check with us to see if we needed anything. Life doesn't get much better than that!

One of our most played games was Monopoly. You never knew what was going to take place when you rolled those dice, and we would sit totally absorbed in the game as if our lives depended upon it. Roll the dice, and you might pass "Go" and collect $200. On the other hand, you might end up in jail. It was all up to the way the dice happened to fall—and how merciful the other player might be.

Board games can be vicious. Just about the time you think that you're getting ahead, someone you thought was your friend makes a move that shatters your hope of winning.

As adults, we still play games, and those games are just as intense and time-consuming as the ones we played so many years ago. Most people play the "work game." As with Monopoly, the work game demands a lot of time and attention, and it also can be vicious. Just when you think things are getting better in your career so that you can pass "Go" and collect $200, something happens, and you miss the opportunity. Then there are those who have a long commute to and from work. These people often play the "time game." Some spend hours every day sitting in their car on the interstate. Very closely related to the time game is the "traffic game." The traffic game offers you the opportunity to sit helplessly still with thousands of cars around you in what seems to be unending torture.

Upon arrival at home, the man who has just finished the "traffic game" is now ready to begin playing the "home game." Totally exhausted, he staggers through the door and begins doing the mundane but necessary tasks of home life. Meals must be prepared, garbage must be taken out, and dishes must be washed. After paying bills, there is the dreaded answering machine. He pushes the "Play" button and discovers that three people have asked for a return call. Then it's time to check the e-mail and to reply.

With little time and energy left, a feeble attempt is made to play the "family game." While our modern-day warrior is on the verge of total collapse, bouncing children demand his full attention. These full-of-life children want Dad or Mom to play with them. There is homework that must be done, and then, as a last duty for the day, parents listen to the problems of their little ones who are depending on them to fix what has been broken in their lives that day.

Those board games I played with my cousin decades ago were much less demanding than the game of life. What do you do when you have given all you can give and there is nothing left? What do you do when your body rebels against what your mind knows you should do, and you are facing "burnout"? One option is to "throw in the towel." It is to become so discouraged that you want to quit. You become disheartened, disillusioned, and unable to go on. It's just too overwhelming, just too much. I am sure that Paul must have felt that way at times, but he learned the secret of overcoming such thoughts:

> Therefore we do not lose heart. Though outwardly we are wasting away, yet inwardly we are being renewed day by day. For our light and momentary troubles are achieving for us an eternal glory that far outweighs them all. So we fix our eyes not on what is seen, but on what is unseen. For what is seen is temporary, but what is unseen is eternal. (2 Corinthians 4:16-18)

The apostle Paul found the secret of longevity in the game of life that he played so well. Simply put, he learned to live a Spirit-filled life with an eternal perspective. He knew that the troubles he faced were only momentary, but those problems were achieving for him a blessedness that would never end. Physically Paul lived in this world. Mentally and spiritually, he lived with his mind set on heaven. Because his mind was fixed on heaven, nothing on earth could cause him to lose heart.

The game of life has changed its form many times in the two thousand years since Paul lived, but the way you win the game has not changed. No one can consistently live with enthusiasm and stay true to God unless he has an inner strength from the Holy Spirit. Being filled with God's Word and His Spirit is a "must do." In the midst of a busy schedule that seems to have no end, drawing from the Well of Life must be prioritized. That is the way you win the game of life.

God, we only have one chance to live the kind of life You have designed for us. Help us not to lose the opportunity to give You praise and glory. We pray in Jesus's name. Amen.

CHAPTER 4

AN IMPORTANT QUESTION

Pictures are marvelous things because they capture a moment in time that will never be exactly the same again. When is the last time you looked at an old scrapbook? You may be surprised at how young your parents looked. It may not be your "best move" to tell them, but they certainly have changed a great deal since the camera captured their likeness those many years ago. Your father had a full head of hair, and your mother was so much thinner. It is amazing what a few years can do.

And then there are the school pictures that were taken of you from first grade through graduation. You look at your first-grade portrait and realize that you were really a cute little kid. You sure looked different back then. My, my, how you have changed! With each passing year, you see yourself becoming older and, hopefully, more mature.

Now that you have travelled down memory lane for a while, I want to ask you a very personal and important question. If you are twelve years old or younger, I am quite sure that you won't mind answering. As you transition between the ages of thirteen to nineteen, you will become increasingly glad to answer. And when you hit twenty-one, you may be downright proud of your answer to this question. Beyond that point, however, things turn south, and you become less thrilled to answer with each passing year.

Yes, you have figured it out. I'm asking you about your age. How old are you? Look again at those pictures in the old scrapbook. How old was your father in that picture? And how old were you when this picture was taken? You may think giving the right answer to how old you are is a very easy thing to do, but it may be more difficult than you think. That's because pictures of your outward appearance don't tell the whole story. If we were to find out where you really are in life, you would have to do more than count your chronological years. You would have to have a camera that could take a picture of your inner man. That is because your real age is not measured by the number of years you have been alive. Your real age is determined by how much life there is in you.

Unfortunately people in our culture seem to be getting older at a faster rate of speed. Children are being swept into the teen culture at an earlier age than ever before. By the time some young people have graduated from high school, they have become old in spirit by indulging in things that drain life rather than add to it. On the other hand, some people who are much older chronologically are brimming over with life and expectancy.

A man named Caleb from the Old Testament was like that. When Joshua took command of the armies of Israel, Caleb said in Joshua 14:10-11, "So here I am today, eighty-five years old! I am still as strong today as the day Moses sent me out; I'm just as vigorous to go out to battle now as I was then." Caleb might have been eighty-five chronologically, but he was not old. If our special camera that takes pictures of the inner person had taken Caleb's picture, we would find that he was young in spirit. How about you? How old are you?

If life has become a meaningless treadmill, then you are as old as the eighteen-year-old high-school graduate who has prematurely aged and become old in his thinking. If, on the other hand, you are filled with the joy of the Lord, you are as young as Caleb was at the age of eighty-five. You see, the real fountain of youth is found in a relationship with the Lord, whereby you live out His plan for your life. It is a life that is lived trusting Him and anticipating His blessings on your obedience.

That being true, neither youth nor old age is strictly a number. Youth is an attitude that is still in the discovery mode. It is an attitude that anticipates the good things God is going to do in your life. In contrast, old age feels that all has been seen and experienced, so life becomes a dull routine. When you no longer have the joy of a growing relationship with God, you are old.

Would you like to live a life of perpetual youth? Then live to please God. In Psalm 103:5, the psalmist says that God "satisfies your desires with good things so that your youth is renewed like the eagle's." The amazing thing about all this is that you can actually decrease in age. That's right. You can be younger in spirit at age fifty than you were at age twenty-five. It's all in the attitude, and your attitude is your choice. The pictures taken of your outward body may record the chronological progression that happens to everyone, but the real you living within the body can actually be more energetic and alive with each passing year. If you want to live a young life, you can. Fill your life with God, and God will fill your life with youth!

God, help us to live our lives focused on You. Renew us within, Lord, that we may do Your work with excitement and the joy of youth. We ask this for Your glory and our good. Amen.

CHAPTER 5

THE LAKE HOUSE

When I was a young boy, one of my uncles had a house on Lake Cherokee. I will never forget the times that my extended family shared together at that lake house. It was great! Inside the house was a pool table and more food than you could possibly think about eating. Outside, tall pine trees surrounded the house, and a hammock hung connected to two of these trees. I became very acquainted with that delightful hammock and spent many blissful times lying in it. I would look up at the peaceful blue sky and be cooled by the gentle breeze coming across the lake. I heard the sound of birds singing and the far-off buzz of boats traveling across the lake. Occasionally I experienced the joy of seeing a fish gracefully jump out of the water and then quickly disappear again. I also enjoyed walking out on the long pier and feeling the sensation of really being on the water. I even tried my hand at fishing, but I found the fish to be very uncooperative.

It was also a very special thing to walk out into the shallow water and go swimming, and sometimes you would see small fish in that surface water. The kids would have a great time, but there was one thing a child had to be careful of. A child could be wading carefully in the shallow water, and suddenly there would be a drop-off, a low point. If one were to walk into the low point, he or she would sink, and sinking is not a good thing to do if you don't know how to swim well. So there were high points and there were low points. That sounds a lot like life, doesn't it?

Life is indeed made up of high points and low points. But most of the time, we're walking on ground that is somewhere between the two extremes.

That medium spot in life is better than the "drop-off" places, but it is not what we want. We want our lives to be full of high points, special times when all is going well, but as much as we might not want it to be, we will at times be plunged into the deep water of circumstances that threaten us and our safety. We want to be able to lie in the hammock of life, to enjoy the breeze of positive circumstances and the delicacies of good times. In other words, we all really want one thing: we want to be happy.

Happiness is a much sought after commodity, but it has a way of eluding us much of the time. Instead of the fun we want, we often step into an unexpected drop-off point in life. We ask ourselves, "Why doesn't God do something to make me happy?' If God loves me, why do I have to live so much of my life in the low points?"

Our biggest problem is in a lack of understanding how to achieve this state of being we call "happiness." What do we do that will allow us to live on the top rather than on the bottom? First, seek to cultivate a close family life. My experiences at the lake house as a child were happy because I was with my family. God created the family, and He wants us to enjoy life together. Second, be a part of a close spiritual family. God delights when His people love one another and enjoy spiritual fellowship together. Last, keep your heart clean. Proverbs 4:23 says, "Above all else, guard your heart, for it is the wellspring of life." Your heart is like a factory that produces everything that comes out of your life. If you are frustrated or angry, those emotions began in your heart.

You are a spiritual soldier with the task of guarding your heart from all that is not pleasing to God. Does self-pity attempt to enter your heart? Refuse to allow it to come in. Does anger try to sneak in? Stop it before it comes. All unbiblical thoughts will lead you to a "drop-off" point in your spiritual life.

My uncle's lake house was filled with happy people, and God wants no less for His people today. It is surprising how many references there are in the Old and New Testaments to delight, joy, and rejoicing. God wants His people to be happy, but that kind of joy comes only as we guard our thoughts and breathe in the air of heaven.

Psalm 32:10-11 says, "Many are the woes of the wicked, but the LORD's unfailing love surrounds the man who trusts in him. Rejoice in the LORD and be glad, you righteous; sing, all you who are upright in heart!" Whether it is the psalm writer, the apostle Paul, or any other godly person, they will all tell you the same thing: walking on the high ground of joy is the product of walking closely with the Lord and sharing his joy with others.

Heavenly Father, we live in a physical world, and it is so easy for us to get our attention on material things rather than to keep our attention on pleasing You. Help us to know that You are and always will be the source of all true joy.

CHAPTER 6

ONLY GOD CAN SATISFY

In Genesis 2:18, God made a profound statement about the well-being of the man he created: "It is not good for the man to be alone. I will make a helper suitable for him." That statement is powerful when you understand man's environment at that time. Genesis 2:8-10 tells us:

> Now the LORD God had planted a garden in the east, in Eden; and there he put the man he had formed. And the LORD God made all kinds of trees grow out of the ground—trees that were pleasing to the eye and good for food . . . . A river watering the garden flowed from Eden . . . .

When God made man, He put him in a garden that was lush and beautiful in every way. Few can even begin to imagine the beauty, peace, and joy that existed in that first home of man. It was a place people only dream about. Nothing was lacking or missing. If beauty, perfection, total safety, and perfect health were enough to give someone a fulfilled life, this first man, Adam, would surely have been overflowing. He had everything. He lived in a perfect environment that was never too hot and never too cold. He had no fear because there was no danger. In the newly formed earth, the man coexisted with animals of all kinds and enjoyed their beauty and company. A huge tiger was as gentle as a little kitten, and a giant wolf was as playful as a new puppy. God's creation was in perfect harmony, and man lived in a utopian society, possessing everything he desired. However, there was still something lacking. As we saw above, God said, "It is not good for the man to be alone." So God created a woman for the man, someone who was like him and yet different. Although many years have passed, it is still not good that man be alone. We need relationships. Our current songs, movies, and books all testify to our need for relationships.

Unfortunately that is as far as many people go. They search their whole lives for that special person who will be able to fill the longing in their souls. They look to parents, children, and other significant people to take away the inner hunger, but none of it works. Even though they may spend a lifetime looking, they are bound to be disappointed. Can a branch bear fruit apart from the vine? Can a light bulb shine without electricity? Can a jet safely land without its landing gear? Neither can a human being be satisfied within apart from the Source, because no other person, no amount of money nor pleasure can fill the God-sized vacuum in the human heart. Mankind was made for fellowship with God, and that need has not been become less with the passing of years. We still hunger within to be close to the Almighty. Does it seem strange to you that God wants a relationship with mortal human beings? After all, at best we are broken and have nothing to offer but our sin. We are flawed and often rebel against God's will for our lives, but God still loves us.

Yes, God loves us and wants a relationship with us. In Jeremiah 30:21, He asked an incredible question: "Who is he who will devote himself to be close to me?" In essence, the Lord asked, "Who will love me enough to want to be intimate with me?" It is the Creator seeking fellowship with the created. It is the Perfect seeking the imperfect. It is the All-sufficient One desiring to live life with the insufficient. To think of such things is beyond our comprehension. We have as much chance of filling the ocean in a glass as we do in understanding God's incredible love. You might ask, "How can this be?" The answer is that God is a God of grace, and grace is always undeserved.

The complexity comes in understanding why God is like He is, and that is something that will have to remain a mystery until we reach heaven. When we enter that land which is fairer than anything we can imagine, things that are mysteries to us now will be revealed. Until that time, we must believe what we know to be true. The truth is that total satisfaction and completeness are impossible apart from our relationship with God. Maybe you have experienced the feeling that something is not quite right, and you have tried to understand what that something is. If you have searched but not found, your search can be over today.

God can and will fill your heart with peace, joy, and fulfillment if you are willing to yield your life to Him. Ask Him to help you to love Him and to desire fellowship with Him, and you will find the answer to wholeness you have been seeking. If you seek, you can be sure you will find.

> *Dear God, we are like sheep who wander away. It takes so very little for us to seek after other gods and put You in second or third place when You always deserve to be first. Have mercy on us and help us to rejoice in who You are and how much You love us. Amen.*

CHAPTER 7

CHOOSE WISELY

I n the movie *Indiana Jones and the Last Crusade*, Jones is in a cave seeking the so-called Holy Grail. It is there that he meets an ancient knight who guards it. The knight says, "You must choose, but choose wisely, for as the true grail will bring you life, the false grail will take it from you." How true to life that scene is, because each one of us has many choices to make. Some of those choices will bless us, while others will rob us of the blessings we could have.

When our Creator designed us, He could have made us anything. If He had chosen, He could have made us some sort of humanoid that simply followed orders without any rational thinking process, but He did not. Rather than make us non-thinking creatures, God made us complex persons that are full of complicated and unique feelings. He created us as beings that have the capability of thinking, of feeling, and of choosing. As we think about something, our emotions give birth to desire, and we choose that which we think will make us the happiest. This capacity to desire and long for something is one of the driving forces in anyone's life, and it will ultimately be responsible for who and what we become. We can desire anything for our lives from the lowest to the highest, and God will allow us to do so. It is desire that causes the criminal to break into a bank and rob it. On the other hand, it was desire that caused Mother Teresa to work with homeless, helpless, and diseased people. Desire can take us to the highest heights, or it can sink us into the lowest of lows. It is our choice.

We might ask why it is that anyone would choose the lesser for his life rather than choosing God's best. It doesn't make any sense to take decisions that will not put us at the "top of our game." Why, for example, would someone willingly choose a weak spiritual life that forfeits the joy of seeing prayers answered in an unmistakable way? Why would someone not want to be a mighty soldier of the Cross and be able to make an impact on this world for God? If the Bible is truly God's Word, why would we be so reticent to spend time reading it, meditating on it, and memorizing it?

The problem lies more in the fact that all too often we choose comfort over commitment. We choose the passing pleasures of this life rather than the eternal blessings that will never pass away. It is not that we don't have holy desires. Philippians 2:13 tells us, "for it is God who works in you to will and to act according to his good purpose." The word "works" in this verse is the Greek word from which we get our word "energy." This verse is telling us that God energizes us to do His will, and His will is defined as being "good." It is not only good, it is perfectly good. To follow God's good purpose, our lives will bring God's blessings to rest upon us. To choose to follow a self-designed plan will ultimately disappoint us and leave us hungry for something more. The problem is that the self-willed course usually seems easier and more attractive. It requires less discipline and often promises immediate gratification. It looks good, but down deep within our souls, there is the conviction of the Holy Spirit urging us to choose God's best.

Knowing those things intellectually is one thing, but deciding to obey God is another. We are dependent on God's power to do what we really know is right. The same God who created us with the ability to desire can strengthen us with the power of His might so that we are able to choose what is best rather than that which is convenient or comfortable.

In Psalm 28:7, the psalm writer said, "The LORD is my strength and my shield; in him, my heart trusts, and I am helped." The truth is that every one of us can have as much of God in our lives as we choose to have. Making the choice to live a disciplined life that puts us continually in the presence of God is not easy, but it is a decision that we will never regret. It is best for us, for our families, and for everyone within our circle of influence. Make it your choice to walk with God in an ever-increasing way. Don't allow the temporary to get in the way of the eternal! Choose, but choose wisely.

Dear Lord, the choices we face are many, and we are often confused. Help us to choose Your way. In Jesus's name, amen.

CHAPTER 8

LIVING ON THE EDGE

A few decades ago, my hometown had a centennial that was a time of celebration like I have never seen before. The streets were full of people and things to do, and every night, the football stadium was filled as the people watched various performances that were orchestrated by a company from California. I will never forget one special night that involved one of my best friends. My friend had become involved with the directors of the show, and someone came up with an idea that totally stunned the crowd. A tall tower was built close to the stands. At first, it was unnoticeable to most because it was in the dark, but it soon had the attention of everyone in the stadium.

Suddenly the stadium lights went out. Music began to play, and a spotlight shone on the top of a tall tower. The spotlight was on my friend, who was standing at the top on the very edge of the platform. There he stood with no shirt and wearing an Indian headdress on his head. The people sat and stared spellbound as if they were one. The questions on the minds of the people sitting in the stadium that night had to be: *What does this mean? What is the reason and meaning of that tall tower? What will happen if he accidentally falls?* He just seemed too close to the edge for safety. That is when the unthinkable jolted everyone to the place of hysteria. My friend began to lean forward and then plunged headfirst toward the ground. The people were on their feet, and screams reverberated throughout the stadium as the people were sure they had just seen a young man plunge to his death. There was, however, a barrel filled with water on the ground, and my friend was soon climbing out of it. It quickly became apparent that this shocking event had been staged. I later asked my friend where he learned to do that. His reply was almost as surprising as his fall. He told me he had never done it before. He had simply seen it done and wanted to try it out for himself.

Many years later, it dawned on me that what happened that night was a good illustration of the way God wants us to live the Christian life. The Christian life is not meant to be lived in a lawn chair while we drink "spiritual lemonade" and munch on "spiritual cookies." The Christian life is meant to be lived on the edge. Living on the edge is not comfortable, because we are afraid that the worst may take place, that we might fall and be hurt. Nevertheless, it is living on the edge that gets the attention of people who need Christ. When are we living on the edge? We live on the edge when God calls us to do something that is potentially hazardous. It is when we walk by faith and not by sight that we're living on the edge.

Abraham knew what it was to live on the edge. When he was seventy-five years old, he was living comfortably in his home surrounded by friends and family in Ur of the Chaldeans. At his age, he probably thought it was time to settle down, time to take it a little slower and easier, to enjoy life. Then God shined the spotlight on Abraham and told him to jump off the spiritual platform he was standing on. Here was a God whom Abraham had never known before, calling him to do something that must have seemed very foolish. Hebrews 11:8-10 tell us:

By faith Abraham, when called to go to a place he would later receive as his inheritance, obeyed and went, even though he did not know where he was going. By faith he made his home in the promised land like a stranger in a foreign country; he lived in tents, as did Isaac and Jacob, who were heirs with him of the same promise. For he was looking forward to the city with foundations, whose architect and builder is God.

God was telling Abraham in his old age to leave all he knew and all he had ever known, and to set out on a journey for a place he had never seen. Can you imagine Abraham trying to explain that to his wife? She was probably concerned for his sanity. That is really living on the edge, but that is what faith is all about. Faith is not sitting in the stands eating popcorn. Rather, faith is standing on the top of a tall tower in the dark, waiting to jump off at God's command and leaving the results up to Him.

Throughout my life, there have been a few times when I have stood on the tall platform and by faith have jumped off into the water. Years ago, I felt God calling me to leave my church family that I dearly loved. I was to load up a U-Haul trailer and move from the familiar surroundings that I grew up in to a huge city for the purpose of starting a new church with zero members, no place to meet, and no money to advertise. I can tell you for sure that it was a struggle, because if I missed the barrel, I would have lost everything. Since that time, I have learned that if God tells me to jump off the edge of a tall tower, then doing so is the safest thing I can possibly do. The danger is never the threatening circumstances. The danger is in not doing God's will.

Many years ago, my friend surprised all of us with something that we would have never thought he would have done. God is still in the business of surprising His people by calling them to do things that they never thought they would or could do. If God is calling you to something way out of your comfort zone, just remember that it is out there on the edge that we experience victories we will never forget the rest of our lives. It is when we are willing to live on the edge that people's lives are impacted. Anyone can sit in the stands, but only people of faith dive off the platform into the water of God's will. Are you one of those people?

Our heavenly Father, we ask You to help us to have the faith and the courage to do what You're calling us to do even though it is not comfortable. We want to see Your fruit in our lives, and we ask You to help us to walk by faith even when it seems dangerous to do so. We pray in Jesus's name, amen.

CHAPTER 9

WILL THE REAL TRUTH PLEASE STAND UP?

When I was a young boy, we watched *To Tell the Truth*, a television show that included three contestants, all of whom were claiming to be the same person. The show's panelists were to ask the contestants questions to determine which one was telling the truth, and then there was that dramatic moment that had been anticipated the whole show. It was the moment of truth when the contestant with the real identity stood up.

The question of truth has been around since the beginning of time. It started in a garden when Satan challenged the truth of God concerning the forbidden fruit. In line with the game show I watched as a child, the real God did indeed show up, and the truth was made known.

People have always had questions about what really constitutes truth. Many years after the Eden story, Jesus was standing before Pilate, and Pilate asked the question, "What is truth?" (John 18:38). The human race has never stopped asking that question. We want to know where our race came from, what we are to be doing, and where we are going. Did an all-powerful deity create the universe, or did it all evolve over the span of billions of years? If a deity is responsible for all that is, who is that deity, and where is He now? Is He involved in our lives, or is He far removed from us? Again, what is truth?

God has actually answered this question throughout history. When the people of Israel were in Egyptian bondage, they cried out to God for deliverance, and God stood up and identified Himself as the truth by sending them a deliverer named Moses. When they came to the impassable Red Sea with Pharaoh's army following in hot pursuit, God once again stood up and said, "I am the truth." Many years later, a baby was born of a virgin, and all of creation shouted praise to the God of truth. That baby grew up to be a perfect man who proclaimed, "I am the way and the truth and the life" (John 14:6). Many have been the times when God has stood up and proclaimed Himself to be the truth. And yet in spite of the great display of truth God has given, we still find ourselves sometimes struggling with unbelief.

Sometimes we doubt because, at the moment, God is not acting the way we had expected Him to act. We wonder why it is that sometimes we pray with all our might and seek to believe God, and all that we get from God is silence. What is truth? Does God really care, and does He hear and answer prayer? We might say with the prophet Elisha, "Where now is the LORD, the God of Elijah?" Or, we can echo the words of the psalm writer in Psalm 119:82, "My eyes fail, looking for your promise . . . ." Like the disciples on the Sea of Galilee (see Mark 4:35-41), we are tossed back and forth by the waves of a terrible spiritual and emotional storm. So, reluctantly, we ask ourselves the question, "What is truth?" If the Bible is really true, where are the answers to our heartfelt prayers? Such is often the plight of good people who struggle to trust God more.

The answer to our frustration, disappointment, and even discouragement is found in the fact that God does things differently than we would because He is God and we are not. He has made it abundantly clear that His ways are not like our ways (see Isaiah 55:8-9).

If we reject His ways and harden our hearts, we are likely to wander in a spiritual desert where the strong winds of a carnal life blow sand into our eyes so that we can no longer see the truth. The children of Israel were in such a situation, and they wandered in circles in the desert for forty years until they died. Only God knows how many Christians have done the same thing.

We must continue our spiritual journey in the midst of circumstances that often don't make any sense and which leave us with more questions than answers because we believe God's Word to be the truth. It is true when we understand it, and it is true when we don't understand it. Truth has stood up in our lives, and we must follow. We don't have to comprehend everything about how a light bulb works for it to illuminate our steps. Neither do we have to understand how God is working in our lives to follow His plan.

Quoting from the Old Testament, the apostle Paul asks a couple of good questions in Romans 11:33-34. He says, "Oh, the depth of the riches of the wisdom and knowledge of God! How unsearchable his judgments, and his paths beyond tracing out! 'Who has known the mind of the Lord? Or who has been his counselor?'" What Paul is saying is that we might need a counselor, but God does not. He is quite sufficient without our advice or instructions. Our goal, then, is to believe and obey His truth found in the Holy Scriptures, knowing that there will come a time on the other side of life when there will be no more mysteries. Our suffering and grief will be understood, and we will praise God that we followed His truth. There are multitudes of ideas and theories in our world, but there is only one truth. Follow it!

*Dear God, please help us to believe You for Jesus's sake
even when we cannot understand. Amen.*

CHAPTER 10

THE TRAIN OF LIFE

When I was about twenty years old, I lived for a short while in Jersey City, New Jersey. Jersey City and New York City were filled with buses, buses, and more buses, which were constantly stopping and starting and emitting great clouds of smoke out of their tailpipes. The sound of horns blowing, the smell of smoke from the buses, and the massive amounts of people all around were new to me. In addition to the buses, there was the continual use of the subway. Up to that point in my life, I had never even seen a subway, so riding one was a first, but not for long. I was able to get a job in the city, and I took the train in every day as transportation to work. The subway, jammed with people, traveled quickly and then slowed down while the conductor announced the name of the street so people would not miss their exit. When the doors opened, people would get off, and others would get on.

Life is like riding a train. All of us begin riding the train of life when we are born, and we travel quickly as year after year passes by. Often, as we ride the train, we meet others who don't share our Christian values. The trains in New York City were filled with people of many different ethnic groups, cultures, and backgrounds, all having their own perspective on life, most of which was not biblical. Today more and more people are departing from the Judeo-Christian ethic and replacing it with a new morality that is really no morality at all. It is the same-old immorality that has existed for thousands of years. As we ride through life with people who don't know Christ, we must be careful to maintain a biblical mind-set. Our thoughts must be God's thoughts, and His ways must be our ways.

Whatever the ethnicity or financial status, whatever the moral standards, the train of life is moving in a predetermined direction. God's train travels on carefully placed tracks designed to take us to His will for our lives. Paul the apostle rode on the train of life, and his "getting off place" was a ministry to the Gentiles so that he became the "apostle to the Gentiles" (Romans 11:13). If he had exited anywhere else, he would have missed God's will for his life, and his memory would have probably faded from the pages of history. In the same way, the apostle Peter had to exit the train at the right place so that he could be the apostle to the Jews. Paul and Peter did great things because they knew which stop to take. Things have not changed. We are all riding the train of life, and becoming a successful Christian is determined by our taking the direction that God has planned for us individually. Someone might ask, "With all the options, how can I know where I should get off? In other words, what is God's will for my life?" As people ride in the subway, there are signs designating different places to go. So what are God's signs for our life's direction?

As simple as it may seem, God often works through a reiterated desire. In other words, God's will is often written within our hearts in the form of a holy desire. Psalm 37:23 states, "If the LORD delights in a man's way, he makes his steps firm."

God is not some tyrant who delights in making His people do things that they have no inclination to do. His will is always the one that ultimately brings the greatest satisfaction.

Someone may ask, "If it is that easy, why do people miss God's will?" All too often, Christians miss God's will because they get off the train at the wrong place, and that does not work. Peter could not have been the apostle to the Gentiles, nor could Paul have been the apostle to the Jews. God had prepared each of them for their particular ministries, and He had prepared in advance the ministries for them. If you take the wrong stop, you may be able to function as a human being, but you will miss the exciting adventure that God has tailor-made for you.

The Scriptures gives us another helpful piece of information concerning knowing God's will. Romans 12:1-2 says:

Therefore, I urge you, brothers, in view of God's mercy, to offer your bodies as living sacrifices, holy and pleasing to God—this is your spiritual act of worship. Do not conform any longer to the pattern of this world, but be transformed by the renewing of your mind. Then you will be able to test and approve what God's will is—his good, pleasing and perfect will.

If you want to know where your stop is, you must first of all present your body as a living sacrifice. Reject the secular philosophies of this world and fill your mind with the Word of God. When you do that, the second verse above says that you will be able to prove what the will of God is—the good, acceptable, and perfect will of God.

What you do, you need to do quickly, because you won't ride the train of life forever. There is coming a time when your pilgrimage on earth will be over, and you will go to meet the heavenly Conductor Himself. At that point, nothing will matter but that you have pleased Him.

Dear God, we know that Your will for us is the best thing possible, but we are weak. We ask for Your strength to not be influenced by the philosophies of man and to be able to experience the blessing of fulfilling Your purpose for our lives. Grant this please in Jesus's name. Amen.

CHAPTER 11

HIDE AND SEEK

The words "Ready or not, here I come!" are familiar to most of us because they form the foundation of a children's game called "hide-and-seek." The title of the game explains its nature. One child closes his eyes and counts to ten while other children hurry to find a hiding place. If a child cannot be found by the seeker, he wins the game. I remember playing that game with my cousins in their family's barn. In that particular game, it wasn't long before all were found except one. Every possible inch was searched, but the missing cousin was not found. It appeared that he had either become invisible or he was no longer in the barn. The reality was that he had burrowed his way through bales of hay and was hiding under them. I am not sure how safe that was, but it was a super hiding place.

Although children often play the game, it is not a children's game alone. In fact, many adults play the game more than children, and they have done so for many years. The game originated with the first two adults on the planet. When they chose to obey the Tempter rather than the Creator, they were afraid and hid among the trees (Genesis 3:8). We play that game when we hide our insecurities from other people through the things we buy or the things that we do. We play the game when we hide from ourselves by making excuses for our wrongdoing. We also still hide from God when we harden our hearts and refuse to not listen to Him. We may be able to hide from ourselves. We might even be successful hiding from other people. We will never, however, be able to hide from God.

When God gets into the game, He always finds what He seeks. Not only does He know where we are, He knows who we are and what we are. Hebrews 4:13 says, "Nothing in all creation is hidden from God's sight."

Children play the game because it is fun, but adults often have a different motivation. For many adults, we play the game of hide-and-seek for the same reason that Adam and Eve played it: we are afraid of God's judgment. There is something about sin that brings fear. Proverbs 28:1 says, "The wicked man flees though no one pursues, but the righteous are as bold as a lion." And 1 John 4:18 says, "There is no fear in love. But perfect love drives out fear, because fear has to do with punishment . . . ." There is something written within our very beings that tells us our sin deserves punishment. That is one of the reasons that many people are stressed out so much of the time. Living with sin in your life produces fear, even if we are only vaguely aware of the sin we are committing.

On the other hand, God's perfect knowledge of us should also be a comfort. He knows exactly what we need to live a full and meaningful life, and He wants to lead us into that experience. He understands when our hearts are broken, and when we feel we have no strength to go on. He sees the longing of our souls to be faithful to Him even when we are struggling with temptation. He sees it all. Psalm 139:1-4 says:

O LORD, you have searched me
and you know me.
You know when I sit down and when I rise;
you perceive my thoughts from afar.

You discern my going out and my lying down;
    you are familiar with all my ways.
Before a word is on my tongue
    you know it completely, O LORD.

My cousin hid where we could never find him, but there is nothing that you could possibly hide from God. It is because He knows us with a perfect knowledge. As Psalm 147:3 says, "He heals the brokenhearted and binds up their wounds." Others may never understand the wounds life has inflicted on us, but God does, and He wants to heal them. Second Corinthians 1:3 says, "Praise be to the God and Father of our Lord Jesus Christ, the Father of all compassion and the God of all comfort . . . ." God is the "Father" of compassion, and He cares what is happening in your life. He seeks for you so that He may bless you.

Sometimes God wants us to play the game differently by taking the role of the seeker. We are told in 1 Chronicles 22:19 (ESV), "Now set your mind and heart to seek the LORD your God." God changes the rules of the game when we seek Him, because He will always be found. No matter what you might be facing, God is ready to be found in all of His fullness. He never goes into hiding. Instead He is waiting to provide your every need. Tell Him about your problems, your fears, and your needs, and praise Him for His compassion.

Lord, we thank You that You have a perfect concern for our lives, and we thank You for Your compassion. Truly You bind up the wounds of the brokenhearted, and we praise You. In Jesus's name, we pray. Amen.

CHAPTER 12

BOLDNESS

Some words naturally convey strong images to our minds. To mention the word "newborn" tends to prompt feelings of warmth and happiness because we normally associate that word with a joyful occasion at the hospital where fathers, mothers, grandparents, and other family members all share the excitement of a new family member's entrance into our world.

Just the opposite is the word "death." Death is the departure of someone who may have been very important and special to us. It speaks of losing a part of our life that cannot be replaced.

The word "boldness" is a word that tends to get our attention because it is something that we all wish we had more of. When we hear the word, we think of people who proceeded to do what was right although doing so subjected them to great danger and perhaps even death.

God's prophets in the Old Testament were bold, fearless people who were not afraid to confront anyone's sin in the name of the Lord. Elijah was such a man. Although Elijah did many things, he is perhaps most often thought of in connection with the showdown on Mount Carmel that he had with the prophets of the false god, Baal. One day, without any warning, Elijah appeared to King Ahab and told the king to gather all the people of Israel, along with the 450 prophets of Baal, on Mount Carmel. That was one man against a whole nation. First Kings 18:20-21 says, "So Ahab sent word throughout all Israel and assembled the prophets on Mount Carmel. Elijah went before the people and said, 'How long will you waver between two opinions? If the LORD is God, follow him; but if Baal is God, follow him.'"

He proposed a simple experiment so the people would know which god was the true God:

> Then Elijah said to them, "I am the only one of the LORD's prophets left, but Baal has four hundred and fifty prophets. Get two bulls for us. Let them choose one for themselves, and let them cut it into pieces and put it on the wood but not set fire to it. I will prepare the other bull and put it on the wood but not set fire to it. Then you call on the name of your god, and I will call on the name of the LORD. The God who answers by fire—he is God." Then all the people said, "What you say is good." (1 Kings 18:22-24)

So they basically said, "You've got a deal." The Baal worshippers went first, and after hours of the false prophets screaming, beating drums, and even cutting themselves in order to get Baal's attention, it became apparent that Baal was nowhere to be found. Then Elijah stepped up to the plate:

> At the time of sacrifice, the prophet Elijah stepped forward and prayed: "O LORD, God of Abraham, Isaac and Israel, let it be known today that you are God in Israel and that I am your servant and have done all these things at your command. Answer me, O LORD, answer me, so these people will know that you, O LORD, are God, and that you are turning their hearts back again." Then the fire of the LORD fell and burned up the sacrifice,

the wood, the stones and the soil, and also licked up the water in the trench. When all the people saw this, they fell prostrate and cried, "The LORD—he is God! The LORD—he is God!" (1 Kings 18:36-39)

However you look at it, that is a fantastic display of God's glory and a wonderful illustration of what it means to be courageous. Are we called to anything less in our modern world? Does God want us to be bold in our stand for Christ among non-Christian people? Why should we be slow to express our faith in the true God to people who are following the false gods of our culture? As Christ followers, we should have an unashamed freedom that allows us to testify to the reality of our Lord.

The kind of boldness Elijah had comes when you care more about God's glory than you do about your own safety. It is a mind-set that is willing to sacrifice because we are filled with a godly jealousy for God's name. The apostles displayed that kind of boldness when they appeared before the Sanhedrin, the same people who were responsible for the death of Christ. They should have been terrified. Instead they spoke boldly: "Now when they saw the boldness of Peter and John, and perceived that they were uneducated, common men, they were astonished. And they recognized that they had been with Jesus" (Acts 4:13 ESV). Seeing this stark contrast as compared to a lukewarm Christian who blends in with the cultural woodwork, these people were "astonished" at the boldness the apostles had to share the message of Jesus. Has anyone ever been astonished or even surprised at the freedom with which you share your faith? Pray that God will give you boldness. Pray that He will make you an Elijah for Him.

God, we fear many things. Take away the fear of rejection and the many other things we fear, and implant within our hearts a holy boldness for You. Amen.

CHAPTER 13

GIVING AND RECEIVING LOVE

P ain is something no one likes and everyone experiences. It is the universal dilemma of mankind. When we think of pain, we often think of a migraine headache, an upset stomach, a broken arm or leg, but pain goes much deeper than that. It is probably true that the greatest pain occurs within rather than without. In some ways, it would be easier to have a broken arm than it would to suffer from a broken heart. Who can adequately describe the inward suffering of another individual? How can we describe a soul that is dark and empty?

As we take the time to observe the lives of those around us, we see broken marriages, rebellious children, and dying parents. We see people who have experienced betrayal from someone they love. People are hurting. As Christians, we have been called to imitate the Lord by throwing a spiritual "life preserver" to those who are sinking. We also must remember that many in our own spiritual family are experiencing emotional pain. Our society is becoming more and more impersonal, but we all still need the human touch. Have you ever noticed that when Jesus healed someone, He often touched that person? Obviously the Savior did not have to touch anyone to heal them physically. The touch was a means of healing the wounded emotions inside. That is because a touch—a warm embrace or a hand on someone's shoulder—says, "I care about you." That is the message we all need to hear: "I care about you." It is no wonder that love has such a large emphasis in Scripture. Romans 12:10 says, "Be devoted to one another in brotherly love. Honor one another above yourselves." Again, in 1 Thessalonians 4:9, Paul said, "Now about brotherly love we do not need to write to you, for you yourselves have been taught by God to love each other." We were all designed with a need to love and to be loved. Where love is absent, pain is present.

In spite of that simple truth, thousands of people all over the world are starving for someone to care. Why is it so hard to have this basic need met? Many times, we fail to receive love because we refuse to give it. In Luke 6:38, Jesus said, "Give, and it will be given to you . . . ." He was stating a principle that works in all areas of life. If you are suffering a lack of love, you make the first move. Do loving, kind things for others. When possible, compliment them. When you concentrate on meeting the needs of others, you will reap what you sow (see Galatians 6:7). Sowing love and concern for others results in the same being given back to you.

Obviously, being the first to reach out with love is not an easy thing to do. We would feel more comfortable if people were affirming their love for us. What is more, there is always the chance that our offer of love may be rejected. We must, through the power of God's Holy Spirit, imitate the One who loves the unlovely. In our imitation of Christ, we can expect to receive what He received. In all likelihood, we will receive a certain amount of rejection, but by His grace, God will ignite the hearts of some who will return your love for theirs. Remember, first give and then receive.

Lord, we cannot give what we don't have, so we are asking You to pour Your love into our hearts so that we can love others. We ask this in Jesus's name. Amen.

CHAPTER 14

COMMON THINGS

Most people have a thirst for the unusual, and yesterday provided just such an environment for me. It was the Fourth of July, and as usual, some incredible fireworks displays evoked sounds of wonder and unbelief among those who anxiously and excitedly watched the show. As the time passed by, the anticipation of people grew more and more intense as they waited for the grand finale. We like the uncommon, the unusual. We are in awe as a stunt man does exciting and dangerous things, or as a circus performer goes into a cage with a dangerous animal such as a lion or tiger.

For some, it is not enough to watch; they want to be involved so they can personally experience the adrenaline rush for themselves. Some risk their lives climbing mountains with an insatiable desire to go higher and higher. One reason we love the unusual is because it takes our mind off the usual.

The usual can become monotonous and boring, and we inwardly hunger for something new and exciting. We want to be catapulted out of the routine of life and to be captivated by something so breathtaking that we will momentarily forget the stress, pain, and confusion we are experiencing. When I was a child, my parents took me to Six Flags over Texas, and I found myself in a totally new world, a world where words like "homework" and "grades" were not mentioned. It was a world where cleaning my room did not exist. Instead I was able to get in a boat and ride down a mystical river where animated creatures were busy doing their jobs, where pirates shot their cannons at the boat, and where a multitude of things continued to amaze those who were lucky enough to be in that "fairy tale" world. We love to be entertained. The truth is, however, that the most important things in this world are not in the category of the unusual. They are in the category of the common.

When God spoke through Paul in 2 Corinthians, He described people as clay pots that light can shine through (see 2 Corinthians 4:6-11). There's nothing extravagant or spectacular about a clay pot, but it becomes important if we allow the light of Jesus to shine through it in a dark world. When Jesus came to earth, He could've come with explosions in the heavens and put on a fireworks show that the whole world would have seen. He could have flown through the sky with light emanating from His body, such as it did in the Transfiguration, but instead He came as a human baby. Not only that, He was born in a manger in a stable to common parents.

One of the problems with the uncommon things that we so desire is that they don't come often enough. Most of our time is spent with the ordinary, but it doesn't have to be that way. God has given us the privilege of living the most extraordinary life possible: a life that is lived in His will. What could be any more exciting than living the kind of Christianity that we see in the New Testament? There was no dullness or "business as usual" with the early church. Rather, there was a sense of excitement and anticipation that filled the air. There was the excitement of seeing people leave their former lifestyles and begin to live a new kind of life. People who were once divided found reconciliation, and Christians used their spiritual gifts to minister to one another.

The kind of motivation that stirs the believer's heart needs no extraordinary circumstances. It is the product of finding God's will and living it out in the fullness of the Spirit. Fireworks may be very exciting, but they cannot be compared to "fireworks" in your soul. It is also an exciting thing to ride down a man-made river about four feet deep and to see mechanical animated figures, but none of those things can come close to being used by God and to be a part of His plan. There is great joy in the common things of life when we place them in the hands of God.

Our Father in heaven, help us to not be bogged down with the routine of life when we could be experiencing the joy of fellowship with You. Draw us to Yourself and use us to draw others to You. Amen.

CHAPTER 15

LIFE IN THE ROCKING CHAIR

When God made us, He gave us the desire to accomplish things, to move ahead, to explore new avenues in life. For many of us, we would like to travel at the speed of light. We want to get to where we're going, and we want to do it quickly. We enjoy seeing the advancement of our lives and the fruit of our efforts. To our dismay, though, more often than not, we find our lives sitting in a sort of "rocking chair." A rocking chair has a peculiar function. It takes you forward, but then it quickly takes you back to where you were. Isn't that like life? With all of our striving to move forward, we often find any gains we make to be short lived. We may go forward in one area of our lives, but we soon find ourselves moving backward in some other area. The rocking chair gives us plenty to do; it just doesn't take us anywhere. So there we sit in life, rocking back and forth and getting nowhere fast.

The rocking-chair life seems to be an exercise in futility, and it brings with it many questions. Why would God put within our hearts a desire to move forward in our lives and then place us in a rocking-chair kind of existence? It seems to be out of sync with His character to willingly subject us to an uneventful, unproductive, and discouraging lifestyle. Maybe the answer lies in the fact that we are moving forward in another way that we don't recognize.

If we were to travel in a fast-moving car, the things we'd pass by would be little more than a blur, giving us little time to examine our surroundings, but that is not the way it is in a rocking chair. The rocking chair forces us to see things that we would not see otherwise. We see, for example, the crack in the molding, the smudge on the door, the tree that needs to be watered, and a host of many other things that we would miss if we were moving at a faster speed.

The rocking chair of life also forces us to be willing to see things in our personal lives that we would not otherwise observe. As we call out to God to deliver us from our meaningless rocking, He reveals to us the selfishness, pride, and anger that, unknown to us, reside in our hearts. The rocking chair may not take us anywhere, but it sure teaches us a lot about our lives. As we cry out to God seeking deliverance, we begin to learn what it is to know Him and trust Him in those unexplainable and seemingly useless setbacks. It is in those times that we learn that God is the supreme pursuit of life. All of our accomplishments and advancements fade into nothingness as we begin to know Him more fully.

The rocking chair of life is really not an exercise in futility or a place of stagnation. Rather it is a means toward the greatest accomplishment possible: a closer walk with God. Advancement physically is a good thing, but advancement spiritually is a great thing. God many times allows us to trade in the good for the best by means of an unlikely tool: a rocking-chair existence.

If we are faithful to learn our lessons well, God may allow us to one day get up out of the rocking chair and to move forward, but if He does, we will not be the same people we would have been had we had not experienced the rocking chair. We will be people who have become strong in faith and who are able to reflect the character of Christ to an unbelieving world. Thank God for the rocking chair.

Lord, please help us to understand that Your ways are perfect, so that we may learn Your lessons well. Amen.

CHAPTER 16

WOODWORK AND A PLANT

A skilled craftsman takes a piece of wood and begins carving. With the greatest of care, he chisels here and there. He cuts the wood until it begins to look like the picture he already has in his mind. When he has finished shaping his masterpiece, he begins applying just the right grade of sandpaper, and what was once only a piece of wood has now become a work of art.

A plant sits near his newly formed reproduction of his mental image, and on the surface, there seems to be nothing special about this plant. It boasts no beautiful flowers or lush green leaves. It is something to be enjoyed by its owner, but it's nothing out of the ordinary. If asked what the difference is between these two objects, you might point to the work that it took to produce the one, as opposed to the plant, which grew on its own. It could be that you would draw attention to the fact that the man's wooden creation has a financial aspect attached to it, and the plant could be obtained freely by anyone. Surely the craftsman's work would be of more value than a plant that cost nothing in terms of effort or price. If all that you see is something that can be bought and sold as in contrast to something that has no such price tag, then you have missed the most important thing. The plant's most important quality is that it has life, and having life gives it the capacity to grow and reproduce. It does not matter how skilled the craftsman may be or how many people like his work, he will never be able to produce life. Life is a gift from God. Read through the opening chapters of the book of Genesis and see Him give life to that which would otherwise be lifeless.

The comparison between the carefully whittled wooden object and the plant endowed with life from its Creator illustrates the difference between religion and Christianity. Since the earliest of times, people have sought to create their own religions. Spiritually speaking, they have "carved" ever so carefully the dictates of their religion. They have clothed it with beautiful ceremonies that leave the worshiper with a feeling of piety and a greater acceptance from God. That may be the perception, but it is not the truth. God is not impressed with our own self-devised religions. He is pleased when someone comes before Him with an attitude of humility and repentance, and a desire to know and love Him more.

An excellent example of religion versus relationship is seen in the life of a good king who brought about religious reform in Judah. Second Kings 18:1, 4 says:

In the third year of Hoshea son of Elah king of Israel, Hezekiah son of Ahaz king of Judah began to reign . . . . He removed the high places, smashed the sacred stones and cut down the Asherah poles. He broke into pieces the bronze snake Moses had made, for up to that time the Israelites had been burning incense to it. (It was called Nehushtan.)

The bronze snake mentioned here had a wonderful place in the history of Israel (see Numbers 21:4-9). When the people sinned in the desert during the time of Moses, God sent snakes to bite and kill them as punishment. He then instructed Moses to make a bronze snake and hold it up, so that whoever looked at it would not die but live. There had been life in that bronze snake, but that was around seven hundred years prior to Hezekiah's life. During the intervening years, the people had actually begun to worship the bronze snake. They were worshipping something that once had life, but which had nothing left but religion. Hezekiah took the object of worship and broke it in pieces.

Unfortunately many of God's people are worshipping a bronze snake. They practice their ceremonies, read their prayers, but receive no spiritual life. They are like those Paul referred to in 2 Timothy 3:5: "having a form of godliness but denying its power. Have nothing to do with them."

Just as it is with the skilled craftsman, we have no power to create life with God. We only have the capacity to yield our lives to Him and to experience the blessing of communicating with Him in our spirits. It is an unfortunate thing that so many lack a vital relationship with God, which alone can bring true joy and real growth.

In 1 John 1:2-4, the apostle John said:

The life appeared; we have seen it and testify to it, and we proclaim to you the eternal life, which was with the Father and has appeared to us. We proclaim to you what we have seen and heard, so that you also may have fellowship with us. And our fellowship is with the Father and with his Son, Jesus Christ. We write this to make our joy complete.

The complete joy that John spoke of is not one that can ever be obtained by creating a masterpiece of religion or worshipping a religious relic such as a bronze snake. It is a gift from God to those whose hearts are inclined to seek Him in spirit and in truth.

Would you say that you have a religious life or a spiritual life? A religious life is done at certain times in certain places. On the other hand, a spiritual life is walking hand in hand with God through the journey of life. It is receiving power from Him to be and to do what He made you to do.

Father in heaven, help us to discern the true from the false, the spiritual from the religious. Help us to walk with You. In the name of Jesus', we pray. Amen.

CHAPTER 17

WALKING IN THE LIGHT

What do flashlights, lanterns, and candles have in common? Yes, they all produce light. In the very beginning, God said, "Let there be light" (Genesis 1:3). God does not do anything that is not important, and light has always been on our own priority list. Without light, life becomes a confusing thing. On more than one occasion, I have gotten up in the night in a dark room and become thoroughly confused as to where I was. The best I could do was to feel my way around the walls and the doorways, hoping to not run into something and be left lying on the floor. Having lived my earlier life in a more rural area, I know the experience of being in a pitch-black pasture, totally lost with no clue about what direction to go. Yes, if one were to drive down the road without light, he or she would soon be in a ditch or, even worse, have a collision with another vehicle.

A pasture can become very dark, but not nearly as dark as an experience that I had years ago. I had flown out to a small town in Arizona to candidate for a start-up church. Very few trees could be seen in the small town, only cactuses and tumbleweeds. I did not know, though, that someone I went to Bible college with lived in that area. When we met one another there, he invited me out to his home to eat his wife's homemade pizza, and I quickly took him up on the offer. As he drove in that Arizona desert, there were absolutely no streetlights of any kind. Even the heavenly bodies refuse to give their light. It was the darkest place I have ever been in my life, and I saw nothing until we approached his home. Left to myself, I would have walked around in circles, stumbling and falling and terrified at the total absence of light.

Light is important. Without it, one cannot safely ride a bicycle, drive a car, or even take a walk. Yet its importance goes further than the physical aspect I have described. Light is also necessary for direction in decisions. Just as I would not know where I wanted to go in a darkened pasture, neither do I know how to make the decisions of life without God's light. God's spiritual and moral light illuminates. It tells us the truth about things and directs our path. It tells us that the direction coming from the world system is faulty and only leads us to ruin. Spiritual life also makes it possible to connect with God.

First John 1:5-6 says, "This is the message we have heard from him and declare to you: God is light; in him there is no darkness at all. If we claim to have fellowship with him and yet walk in the darkness, we lie and do not live by the truth." There are many in our world who claim to know God, but it is living in the light of God's Word that proves we know Him and that identifies us with Him. Living by God's light also displays His glory through our lives. The Old Testament word for "glory" refers to the shining light of God's presence that led the people of God through the wilderness. Later, it was the light that filled the tabernacle. Today it is God's glory shining through us that gets the attention of the world and proves His existence in an undeniable way. For example, take a person who is filled with selfishness, a person who seems to have no morality and whose value system is based upon material things, and then see that person transformed into a selfless servant of God. Such a transformation shouts the truth that God is a glorious being and that He does glorious things.

One of the downsides of some sources of light is that they begin to lose their strength over a period of time. Light bulbs can become old and cease to shine. The starry sky positioned against the brightness of the moon can be eclipsed by dark clouds. Dark clouds even have the power to hide the sun so as to create dark, gloomy days. Light that becomes dim loses its capacity to do that which it was created to do.

The same is true in matters of the spiritual. For example, God wants His church to unveil the truth of his glory because it shines with his light. On the other hand, a church composed of people who are not walking closely with their Lord is not able to attract anyone. It becomes of little more value than a secular organization that may do humanitarian work.

That kind of church may have a name that says it lives when it is really dead. In order to be a living and thriving church, it must be continually recharged by the Holy Spirit working through the light of His Word. The desire of the redeemed should be like the heart cry of the psalmist in Psalm 108:5, "Be exalted, O God, above the heavens, and let your glory be over all the earth." Changing the wording, we could say, "let your light shine throughout the earth."

How about you? Is the light of God within you shining in an ever-increasing way? Are people who see you attracted to the One who is creating the light in your life, or has the light within you begun the process of decreasing so that you appear to be little different from those who do not know Christ?

If you find that your light has become dim so that you are no longer illuminating the darkness around you, cast your whole self on God and ask Him to forgive and renew you.

In 2 Corinthians 4:16, Paul said, "Though outwardly we are wasting away, yet inwardly we are being renewed day by day." It is the daily renewal before the face of God that enables us to shine as lights in the universe and to bring glory to the Source and Sustainer of all that is.

Dear God, how often we fail to recognize the need to recharge our lights. How easy it is to let the light within us begin to dim slowly but surely, like a dimmer switch on a light that can be turned down. We ask You to help us to have the discipline to read Your Word and to listen to Your voice. Help us to learn to pray that we may communicate with You and shine as a result of that communication.

CHAPTER 18

THE BIG HOUSE

Throughout my younger years, which were often filled with change and uncertainty, I had one symbol of stability for many years: the Big House. When you read those words, you no doubt think of a house that is being described as big. When my family hears those words, we do not think of a noun preceded by an adjective. We think of a dwelling place that is precious to all of our hearts. It was first built by Dr. A. O. Menifee (my great-grandfather), and it is the place where my grandmother and her sister Agnes lived after he passed away.

The Big House was not just a residence were two ladies lived. It was the center of our family life. It has been said that in the Old Testament, Jerusalem was the center of Israel, and the center of Israel was the Temple. In like manner, the Big House served as the center of my large extended family. It was a very big colonial-style home with huge white pillars on the front porch and a redbrick sidewalk that began on the left side of the house, covered the entire front, and even extended out to the main highway. In addition, it was originally equipped with balconies for the family to sit out on and enjoy the view. It had a large screened-in back porch and a big backyard that extended down to the home of one of my aunts.

More important than its architectural structure was the fact that it was a meeting place for family life. Everything revolved around the Big House. Easter, Thanksgiving, the family Christmas party, Christmas Eve, Christmas Day, New Year's Day—all holidays were spent with my extended family at the Big House. That meant a lot of people and a lot of food. On those special days, maids were hired to cook huge meals, and they really knew how to cook! I'm talking about Southern-style meals—you know, mashed potatoes with gravy, fried okra, fresh tomatoes, beef roast, unbelievably good rolls, green beans, squash, black-eyed peas, corn bread, and plenty of desserts: pecan pies, apple pies, chocolate pies, and more and more. The Big House made special days pretty predictable. You didn't have to think about what you were going to do; you knew exactly what you were going to do: you were going to the Big House to join all of the other relatives there.

Christmas Eve was a sight to behold because in that large family, everyone gave everyone else a present that was placed under a huge Christmas tree in one of the rooms near the living room. The tree reached the ceiling in height, and the presents were so many that they were stacked one on top of the other but still flooded out of their room into the entrance of another room. So there we were together every Christmas Eve to see our family and to receive the gifts to be given to us.

But I can't forget another important part of the Christmas Eve celebration. Before the packages were opened, each one of the children had to perform for the adults. That was both good and bad—good for the adults but bad for the children, who never wanted to perform, but perform they would. As the adults watched and listened attentively, each child did his thing. My cousin would play the piano. I would sing "Silent Night," and others would do his or her own special performance. And after each child performed, there would be an outburst of applause and praise from the adults. In fact, the clapping and the verbal affirmations didn't stop at once. All of it just sort of faded out after a few minutes of fervent compliments.

It was as if these children had just done something akin to saving the world from some serious disaster. Surely they were all destined to greatness on some concert stage someday. They were child prodigies, little geniuses who had not yet been discovered by the world at large. If the news media had only known what those children were capable of, the youngsters would have no doubt been on television, enjoying huge contracts and immense popularity.

When the performances were over and the last nervous child had just completed his mandatory talent act, the children could breathe easier, calm down, and wait for the main event: the opening of packages. It was a "One, two, go!" kind of thing. Suddenly the air was filled with Christmas wrapping as children devastated boxes in order to get to the prize within them. All the while this explosion was taking place, concerned parents were asking the children, "Now who gave you that?" That's because the recipient of gifts was expected to write thank-you notes to the giver, a thing that would be impossible to do if all the gifts were mixed together with no tags. The festive occasion seemed to last forever, but after a long night of celebration, parents and children loaded up their cars and took their bounty home.

The next morning, the children woke up in their own homes on Christmas to receive another truckload of gifts under their Christmas trees. The most favored of those gifts would then be transported back to the Big House so that all the other family members could see what Santa Claus had brought them. And, yes, another feast day was in order.

The greatest thing about the Big House, however, was the solidarity it gave to the family unit. If you ever had any doubt about someone loving you, that doubt would quickly disappear because you knew there were a whole lot of family members who loved you dearly. You knew that at any time you wanted, you could drive to their homes and be welcomed in as an honored guest, and it all revolved around the Big House. My grandmother was the driving force behind it all. I remember quite well driving up and parking the car at the Big House. Before we could get out of the car, my grandmother was out the door, waiting on us with outstretched arms. She was welcoming, gracious, loving, and kind, and she passed her love and hospitality down to the rest of the family. In addition to her love, she possessed a heart that was dedicated to serving God. Her faith was no doubt passed down to her by her father, Dr. Menifee, who had served as an elder in the Presbyterian church in Tatum for many years. I remember seeing her devotional books and seeing her read them at night, and Billy Graham was a prime attraction.

As children, we knew that if we did not want to watch Billy Graham when he came on television, we had better be somewhere where my grandmother couldn't find us. If we were spotted anywhere, it was time to come in and listen to the evangelist.

The years have come and gone, and my grandmother is no longer with us. She and her two sisters are now in the presence of the Lord. As great as the family unit was and as great as the Big House was, their eyes now see something greater. They see something that we can only vaguely imagine. They are now in a place where there is no sin, no suffering, and no sorrow. Never again will they see one of their family members pass away. Never again will they take that trip to the cemetery to say their last good-byes, because there are no good-byes where they are. There is only joy unspeakable and fullness of glory in a city that is filled with the kind of love that emanated from my grandmother.

Today the big house stands empty. There are no more joyous occasions, no more parties, no more feasts, no more children excruciatingly going through their prepared performances, no more parents raving over how well the children did. That is all over, but the Big House remains as an illustration of what God wants His family to be. Yes, I was part of the family, but knowing Jesus Christ has placed me in an even larger family—the family of God. Just as it was back in those early days of my life, there are some in the family who are older and others younger, but we are all brothers and sisters bound together by the Holy Spirit who lives within us. Back in the days of my youth, we had a huge exchange of gifts for one another. God also has gifts that He wants us to give to one another. Romans 12:4-8 says:

> Just as each of us has one body with many members, and these members do not all have the same function, so in Christ we who are many form one body, and each member belongs to all the others. We have different gifts, according to the grace given us. If a man's gift is prophesying, let him use it in proportion to his faith. If it is serving, let him serve; if it is teaching, let him teach; if it is encouraging, let him encourage; if it is contributing to the needs of others, let him give generously; if it is leadership, let him govern diligently; if it is showing mercy, let him do it cheerfully.

Do you get the picture? As God's household, we are to be a closely knit family of people who sincerely love one another and minister to one another with the spiritual gifts God has given us. We are a family, a family that is on the same road and traveling to the same destination. In John 14:2, Jesus said, "In my Father's house are many rooms; if it were not so, I would have told you. I am going there to prepare a place for you." The Big House was great, but Jesus is preparing for us a "Big House" that far surpasses the one that I knew as a child. Yes, one of these days, we will step out of this realm of physical existence and enter into the spiritual realm that is greater by far. Instead of red brick to walk on, we will walk on the streets of gold. There will be no need of balconies because we will be able to see as far as we want. And there will be no need to listen to Billy Graham invite people to come to Christ, because everyone in that glorious place will be a follower of Christ. In fact, our entire environment will be a spiritual one. That means no foul language or cursing. There will be no display of anger or violence toward anyone, and although we would have just arrived an earth moment earlier, we will have a sense that this is where we belong. This is the place that we were created to live forever. Our wildest imaginations can only begin to fathom the beauty of this place. As we observe some of earth's beautiful places and realize that the world is under a curse, then what must heaven be like? Once having arrived there, we will never want to leave. We currently know the joy of being in the presence of the Lord on a very limited scale. What will it be like when the heavenly city is filled with the presence of God all the time? You will listen to the angels singing praises to the great King . . . observe the beauty of the jewels as they sparkle and the gates to the city, each one being made of a huge pearl . . . listen to the living creatures as they cry out "Holy, holy, holy." You will feel totally safe, totally secure, totally fulfilled in a way that you never were in your previous life on earth.

And, finally, to be able to see the One you loved having not seen Him and to be able to realize with deepened appreciation what He did for you when He died as your offering for sin. The grandest choir accompanied by the most fantastic orchestra on earth will be nothing more than a monkey beating on a tin bucket with a stick in comparison to the perpetual music in your heart. Only with the aid of the Holy Spirit can we begin to understand these concepts, because they belong to another world not made with hands but spoken into existence by the Almighty One. One day, those whom you have said good-bye to, perhaps good friends or family members, will once again be reunited with you in an existence that is beyond our capacity to imagine. We will all live together in God's Big House. That is something invaluable that we have to look forward to.

Lord, thank You for people You place in our lives who love us and who are examples to us. Amen.

CHAPTER 19

DRIVING DOWN GOD'S FREEWAY

Many things were different in the ancient world, not the least being people's mode of transportation. In simpler times, people either walked or rode on an animal to get to where they were going. That is so far removed from most people in our Western culture that it is hard to relate to. We rarely ever ride donkeys, camels, or even horses for transportation. We are too sophisticated for that. Instead we normally drive cars to our destination points. Whether or not that is good or bad in your estimation depends upon your age, the distance you have to drive, and the condition of the traffic. If you are young person and just beginning to drive, the opportunity to do so is one that is welcomed with open arms. There is a thrill in being able to drive, but that thrill soon leaves us, and driving become something akin to cleaning the house, mowing the yard, or trimming the bushes. It is a necessary evil and something that we're no longer in love with, and yet in most cities, we are left with few options. Walking to work is often out of the question. Riding a bicycle is fine if you're a young person exploring your neighborhood, but you don't want to be an adult taking a bicycle to go grocery shopping. So you drive.

Living in a big city takes driving to a completely new level, as we compete with other drivers for the best positions on the road. Driving in those conditions takes skill because there is always going to be that one person who thinks that he can somehow dart out of his lane and jump in front of you in order to gain five seconds on his trip home. And then there is the tired person who can hardly keep his eyes open, and you find him drifting into your lane. In times of lesser congestion, you find people who envision themselves as race-car drivers whose goal it is to pass every car that they can. One of the key elements in preserving your life in such scenarios is to keep looking ahead and stay in your own lane and to not make any impulsive moves. The same is true with the trip of life.

God has given each of us a route to travel. That route is the will of God for your life, and if you travel in His will, you will have the best driving experience possible. Ephesians 2:10 tells us, "For we are God's workmanship, created in Christ Jesus to do good works, which God prepared in advance for us to do." God has a destination already prepared for you, but you have to travel on the right roads to get there. A Christian who leaves God's will can, at the very least, expect to miss God's best for his life. Unfortunately it can become much worse. There are thousands of Christians who have not only forfeited God's best, they have also found themselves in a serious wreck that sometimes has repercussions that last a lifetime.

When you get in the car of life, there are only a few things you can do. First, you can wait. Sometimes in a big city, the freeway ceases to be a means of transportation and becomes a parking lot. No one likes sitting in bumper-to-bumper traffic, and no one likes sitting still in life, but sitting is just as much a part of God's will as moving. When Saul of Tarsus (later called Paul) came to Christ, God sent him out to the desert of Arabia for three years in order to prepare for his ministry. If God does not seem to be moving you forward, consider the fact that He may be wanting you to learn valuable truths that require you to sit still. Many times, God wants you to stay in the lane you are already in. You are on the right road, so stay on it. Sometimes you are tempted to change lanes because your lane is not moving fast enough. Remember, if it is God's will for your life, He knows what is ahead. Traveling down His road will get you where you need to be faster than any other road can. So you can sit still. You can travel straight ahead in your own lane, and sometimes you need to change lanes. You've gone as far as you can go down your present lane, and God wants you to make some changes. Sometimes you come to a dead end. When the time comes to change lanes, God will put on a divine blinker in your heart that tells you which way to go. Colossians 3:15 tells us to "Let the peace of Christ rule in your hearts, since as members of one body you were called to peace. And be thankful."

The peace of God within your heart is His stamp of approval on what you are doing. It is the removal of that peace that tells us we have moved into the wrong lane. It is also necessary for us to listen to God speak to us about things to come. I have a GPS that I sometimes use in my car to give me directions. It is not uncommon to be driving down the road when suddenly the lady in the box speaks and tells me that I have five more miles to go and then I'm to turn right. The Holy Spirit sometimes begins to move on our hearts to prepare us for a coming lane change. The time to change lanes has not come yet, but He is preparing us for the change when it does occur. We must always remember that it was God who put us in the driver's seat, and He rides with us until we go to the place where we will need no cars. One of the key elements in the drive through life is to recognize that His presence is with us, and to draw close to Him in intimate fellowship. That is because His will is not found in a formula. It is found in a relationship. As God is directing us, we will know when it is time to change lanes. That is often not an easy process, but it is one that He will guide us through. Proverbs 16:1 says, "To man belongs the plans of the heart, but from the LORD comes the reply of the tongue." God says, "Put your mind in gear. Listen for any divine blinkers in your heart. Think about what you should do, and I will guide you."

Dear Father, life can be so unsure, and we can easily miss the way.
Please help us to continue in Your will and make the changes You want
us to make plain and clear. We pray in Jesus's name. Amen.

CHAPTER 20

THE STORM

I f you were able to give someone any present you wanted to give, what would it be? Would you give him a new car, a new house, or a second house out on the lake? Maybe you would choose to buy that special person his own jet along with a lifetime supply of fuel. Someone receiving such a gift would be elated.

Can you imagine the look on his face as he tried to fully comprehend your gift? As exciting as that kind of gift would be, it is not close to being the best gift you could give. All the riches in the world do not have the power to stop the gnawing feeling in your heart that something is not right. Try as you may, you will not be able to calm the storm that is going on within. That reminds me of an experience I had as a child.

My family was living in a seemingly peaceful small town, but it was far from being peaceful, because at any time, day, or night, you might be summoned by a loud siren to go to a storm cellar to be protected from a tornado, and my family made many trips to an underground shelter. I vividly remember one time when the siren was blowing in the morning hours. I was lying in the bed half asleep, and the half that was asleep did not want to get up. My dad was frantically trying to wake me up, and as a last resort, he took off his belt. I knew what that meant, and I suddenly felt really motivated to get out of the bed. Living in that little town was not the last time I experienced a storm. Later I was living in Houston when Hurricane Katrina showed its power by destroying everything in its path. Large trees were uprooted, and houses were shattered as Katrina flexed her muscles.

Thankfully such massive displays of nature's wrath are not common experiences, but the storm that resides in the hearts of thousands of people is all too common. Many live daily with a roaring hurricane in their souls. For some, the storm comes from a dysfunctional family. For others, the storm brings tension and strife to a couple who once pledged their love at a marriage altar. Others experience the strong wind of a job crisis. Many kinds of storms rob us of the tranquility we so desperately need.

The answer to this dilemma cannot be purchased or earned. It can only be given by the Creator. An illustration of the storms that so often plague our souls is found in Mark 4:35-41. Jesus and His disciples were in a boat on the Sea of Galilee going to the other side when suddenly the waters became a fierce storm. The disciples, who were trained, seasoned fishermen, had no doubt weathered many treacherous storms, but this one was different. Its power exceeded anything they had ever experienced. The Scripture says,

> Jesus was in the stern, sleeping on a cushion. The disciples woke him and said to him, "Teacher, don't you care if we drown?" He got up, rebuked the wind and said to the waves, "Quiet! Be still!" Then the wind died down and it was completely calm. He said to his disciples, "Why are you so afraid? Do you still have no faith?" (vv. 38-40)

How could Jesus sleep during such a crisis? Jesus could sleep because the things that are so threatening to us, don't threaten God at all. No horrible storm, no sickness or financial setback makes Him the least bit tense. Why should it? He controls everything. The problem lies not with God's ability but with our lack of faith. Observe that Jesus did not rebuke His disciples for not being more skilled at controlling the boat or for not trying hard enough. He rebuked them for their unbelief. They had seen their Master do great miracles before, but they had short memories.

Isn't that the case with us? If you are like most Christians, God has shown Himself to you many times, and yet we doubt when a new threat arises. We tend to default into an unbelieving state of mind, and it is that unbelief that keeps us from having God's best. Hebrews 4:1-2 tell us the sad story of the Israelites in the desert who were not able to go into the Promised Land because they lacked faith:

> Therefore, since the promise of entering his rest still stands, let us be careful that none of you be found to have fallen short of it. For we also have had the gospel preached to us, just as they did; but the message they heard was of no value to them, because those who heard did not combine it with faith.

The "rest" mentioned in verse 1 is a "faith rest," and it gives us the ability to face terrible storms in life as we rest in the promises of God. Believing God enables one to experience a peace that transcends all understanding (see Philippians 4:7). That kind of peace has no logical explanation. It is the result of a choice to make God your refuge, your hiding place, your divine storm cellar. What a great gift!

Father, we are often fearful over many things. We fret and worry when we should be trusting in You. Because You are merciful, we ask You to teach us to truly believe in a way that will bring glory to You and serenity to our souls. Amen.

CHAPTER 21

ACCOUNTABILITY

My parents wanted me to excel in school, and they must have been really disappointed when I didn't. But don't feel sorry for them. Feel sorry for me. They put me through an interrogation process that has seldom been equaled in the history of the world. They wanted to know why I was not doing better. They knew there was nothing wrong with my mind, because I was a very good student until about the fifth grade. When we had spelling contests, I would usually win. If the teacher assigned reading material and later gave a test, I would likely make an "A."

If I had been mentally challenged, my parents would have accepted it, but that wasn't the problem. Knowing what was to come on those dreaded days of interrogation made me sick at heart, and I felt like running away. To this day, although many years have passed, the very phrase "report card" has a negative implication. I imagine that report-card day was far different for those who had diligently done their work and earned good grades. Report cards for those students would have been a time of triumph, a welcomed reward for a job well done. As I mentioned, early in my scholastic career, I knew something of that kind of rejoicing because my grades were high. Those were days when report cards brought praise, and my parents thought of the great things I would one day do. But some good things come to an end. The summer before the sixth grade, we relocated to another city. That is when a lot began happening that sent my grades south. Praise and peace vanished life a puff of smoke, and I dreaded report-card day like one would fear a deadly virus. I knew that when my grades were revealed, I would be punished in the worst possible way: I would be grounded for the entire next six weeks.

I was like someone being held captive as a prisoner of war. Report-card time was a disaster for me. Maybe it could be best understood with terms taken from the Bible: weeping and wailing and gnashing of teeth. I literally had to turn into a hermit. I could not talk on the telephone, watch television, or do anything that would sustain life for a boy my age.

The word "accountability" covers a lot of ground. We are accountable to parents, to teachers, to the legal system, but those do not represent our greatest accountability. Our greatest accountability is to God. He holds us responsible to obey His laws, and He will call us into account for how we have obeyed Him. Romans 14:11-12 says, "It is written: 'As surely as I live,' says the Lord, 'every knee will bow before me; every tongue will confess to God.' So then, each of us will give an account of himself to God." Those words are among the most serious words that can be spoken. Our accountability before God does not mean that we will all stand in one big group and be asked a few general questions. The Scripture knows nothing of such a "crowd judgment." Just as God loves us individually and fellowships with us individually, He will also judge us as individuals. Romans 14:10 says, "For we will all stand before God's judgment seat." It appears from Scripture that the judgment seat of Christ will be very specific and personal. In fact, God will judge more than actions. He will judge the motives behind the actions.

Proverbs 16:2 says, "All a man's ways seem innocent to him, but motives are weighed by the LORD." And 1 Corinthians 4:5 says,

"Therefore judge nothing before the appointed time; wait till the Lord comes. He will bring to light what is hidden in darkness and will expose the motives of men's hearts. At that time each will receive his praise from God." To think that we will have a private audience with God as He reviews our actions, thoughts, and motives is more than our little minds can comprehend.

How will we feel when we are able to clearly see how we chose not to obey God, how we chose to miss opportunities that were never recovered, and how we often did good things for the wrong motives? And all the while, God was ever so patient, giving us chance after chance to change our ways and to embrace His perfect will for our lives.

The most astounding thing about it all may be the fact that God will reward us for the small percentage of our lives that was really lived for Him out of pure motives. Truly our God is a merciful God! It is no wonder the psalmist wrote in Psalm 48:1, "Great is the Lord, and most worthy of praise."

Understanding the unavoidable truth of our accountability to God should cause us to live differently. It should drive us to live a life that seeks to do everything we do to please Him.

Six weeks seemed like a long time to me when the new six-week period began, but each week raced by until I was once again called to give an account to my parents. In the same way, giving an account to God for our lives may seem like it is light years away, but it is not. This present life is flying by us, and soon, dear reader, you will be before your God giving an account for your earthly life. Decide today to live your life for that coming time when all will be revealed.

Lord, we don't know how to respond to this overwhelming truth. It seems so far away, and yet we know that it is near. Please convict us of our wrong and motivate us to do right. In Jesus's name, we ask it. Amen.

CHAPTER 22

TEACH ME, LORD

Psalm 25:4 says, "Show me your ways, O LORD, teach me your paths." Have you ever asked the Lord to teach you? From Genesis to Revelation, the Bible is full of examples of God teaching His people. God speaks to us and teaches us, but I'm not sure how many of us would sign up for the class if we knew what the curriculum was. It is true that God many times speaks to us like a gentle dove as we meditate on His Word. I suppose if it were left up to me, that is where I would leave it. I can deal with a gentle dove, but God often has to speak more loudly, like the noise that would be generated from a fierce storm. It is through those tumultuous storms that we often learn the most about ourselves and about God.

Years ago, I graduated from school with the intention of going to a church to start my dream of being a pastor. I did not know it, but God knew that I needed more education. I am not talking about the kind of education that is found in the classroom. God's seminary is attended in life's hardest circumstances. Surprisingly there were no churches knocking at my door, and without any money to support my family, I had to get a job. Knowing that I was going to leave as soon as I was called to a church, I had no option but to take jobs that someone could get if they were breathing and able to walk and talk. So instead of holding a Bible in my hand, I held a shovel, a pick, a jackhammer, and a clay spade. Instead of wearing a suit and ministering to people, I worked with a group of men who were not interested in being ministered to. I will have to say that they had amazing skills in the area of linguistics. They were able to take words that were normally only used in the crudest ways and fit them together so that they formed sentences. These were truly talented men!

Although I did not realize it at the time, God was interpreting His Word to me. I was being taught what pruning meant. In John 15:1-5 (ESV), Jesus said:

"I am the true vine, and my Father is the vinedresser. Every branch in me that does not bear fruit he takes away, and every branch that does bear fruit he prunes, that it may bear more fruit. Already you are clean because of the word that I have spoken to you. Abide in me, and I in you. As the branch cannot bear fruit by itself, unless it abides in the vine, neither can you, unless you abide in me. I am the vine; you are the branches. Whoever abides in me and I in him, he it is that bears much fruit, for apart from me you can do nothing."

If you had asked me to do so, I could have quoted that passage to you with ease and comfort because I knew it well. The truth is, however, that there is nothing easy or comfortable about what Jesus was trying to teach His disciples and us.

Pruning means something is going to be cut off. Jesus is telling us that sometimes He has to take a sharp knife and cut some things out of our lives that are keeping us from being as productive as we could be. As He cuts, we scream out in pain. Then we see Him looking at another branch that is dear to our hearts, and we say, "No, Lord, not that one!" Surely the Lord would not take that branch, but it is not long before we see the branch falling to the ground. When you prune a branch, you are giving another branch the opportunity to bear more fruit. Do you see that branch in your life that was not very fruitful? With the other branches cut off, it is now showing fruit that it never had before. Do you see the leaf of holiness growing? That pleases the heavenly Gardener because He wants us to be holy so that we can bear His image. Look at that branch again, because there are more new leaves on it.

There is the leaf of humility that was never there before. Proverbs 15:33 says, "The fear of the LORD teaches a man wisdom, and humility comes before honor." It is a humbling thing when God begins to take away some of the things that you are proudest of in your life. Humility comes when you go to Bible school and get a degree so that you can dig ditches. As we saw above, Jesus said in John 15 that without Him we can do nothing. The leaf of humility grows when you began to understand that you cannot do it by yourself. And do you see that leaf next to humility? It is a leaf of ministry. Next to it grows the leaf of a deepened walk with God in prayer and the study of His Word. The pruning that hurt you so badly drove you to seek the Lord as never before. And now you are discovering your spiritual gifts and are using them to serve the Lord for the good of His people and the glory of His name.

Now let's go back to the words of the psalmist that we saw in the beginning: "Show me your ways, O LORD, teach me your paths" (Psalm 25:4). Do you really want the Lord to teach you? If your answer is "Yes," then you should expect some pruning to take place. When it does, don't resist the pruning knife. Be a willing student and be thankful that you have a God who is willing to be your personal tutor. And don't expect to understand all that He is doing. John 13:7 says, "Jesus replied, 'You do not realize now what I am doing, but later you will understand.'" Those things that are now mysteries will one day become clear, and we will understand why God cut off one branch and left another. God knows exactly what branches are hindering your fruitfulness and which branches need to bloom.

Our Father, we know that You do all things right. We may not understand, but we can rest in the assurance that You do. Give us the desire to be taught by You, and help us to be quick learners.

CHAPTER 23

FRIENDS

Words are incredibly powerful symbols that we use to communicate with one another. So strong are they that we can experience deep emotions by simply hearing certain words. For example, how do you feel when you read the following list of words? Training, barber, policeman, death, supervisor, athlete, felon, teacher, lawyer, friend. Which of those words give you a negative feeling? Which word is the most positive to you? It is likely that you would choose the word "friend" as the most positive word. Friendship is a special thing. It starts early in our lives when we find that we like playing blocks with another little child. As you graduate to another level of life and happen to be a little boy, you can shoot marbles, or play with your army men or *Star Wars* figures while at the same time producing the sound effects of gunshots, hand grenades, and crashing jets. If you are a little girl, you can play dolls and dress-up. The years fly by, and soon the little boys are riding bikes together, shooting BB guns, and catching tadpoles or lizards. Little girls are busy deciding what color they would like their hair to be and how different styles would make them beautiful. As time continues its forward march, teenage boys are involved in such things as playing football, lifting weights, and making sure they are drinking their protein shakes. On the other hand, teenage girls are discussing the latest styles of clothing and chattering together about that "cute" boy at school or at church.

As Father Time continues to sweep us along, young men in their early twenties are preparing for their future careers while their female counterparts are busy talking about their dream wedding. Move ahead somewhere forty or more years, and friends—both men and women—spend time together discussing their latest aches and pains and what the doctor told them at their last appointment. And so it goes year after year, with each succeeding year seeming to pass by more quickly, and through it all, we have our friends.

Friends are also "sounding boards," people to whom you can "unload" all of the heartbreaks, frustrations, and hurts that have been thrust upon you by unkind people who seem to want to make your life miserable.

You know you can share those painful things with your friend because he would never do anything to hurt you. You know he can be trusted to jealously guard your reputation.

Friends are normally people who share our values and who enjoy doing things that we enjoy. Friendship takes place when two people "click." Friends also build one another up. You can go to your friend when you are discouraged, and he will encourage you and affirm you. You go discouraged to see your friend, and you leave encouraged. Oh happy alteration!

One famous friendship found in the Bible is the one that existed between David and Jonathan. First Samuel 18:1-4 says:

> After David had finished talking with Saul, Jonathan became one in spirit with David, and he loved him as himself. From that day Saul kept David with him and did not let him return to his father's house. And Jonathan made a covenant with David because he loved him as himself. Jonathan took off the robe he was wearing

and gave it to David, along with his tunic, and even his sword, his bow and his belt.

Look especially at the words "Jonathan became one in spirit with David, and he loved him as himself." To love someone as yourself is to be just as concerned about your friend's needs as you would if you were having those needs. Friends don't close their eyes and walk away when one has a need. If you have a friend, his needs become your needs. When King Saul was seeking to take David's life, David told Jonathan what was going on, and Jonathan said to David, "Whatever you want me to do, I'll do for you" (1 Samuel 20:4). Jonathan was a true friend to David, and he was willing to do anything he could to help his friend. That is true friendship.

True friendship runs deep, and it doesn't come easily. It is the product of patiently enduring the other person's faults. It requires forgiveness and unconditional love. The greatest friend we have is the Friend of sinners who died in our place. John 15:13 says, "Greater love has no one than this, that he lay down his life for his friends." Jesus set the standard for what a friend should be like by laying down His own life for those He called His friends. My experience tells me that you will have plenty of companions in your life. You will have a few who are more than your average friend, but very few, if any, who will be of one spirit with you and who will do anything they can to help you. If God blesses you with such a "soul mate," never take it for granted. Instead nurture and cherish the relationship because you have been given one of God's greatest treasures. Do not allow anything to separate your heart from the heart of your friend. Rather, guard the special bond that you have with that person.

There is something innately born within us that needs companionship, and some are blessed enough to have a special person who can provide that companionship. The truth is, however, that the best and closest human friends you can have are not enough. Our greatest need is to have a friendship with God, our Creator. I admit that it is very difficult to conceive of such a thing.

How can we as limited, finite creatures do anything that would even remotely look like we could have such a relationship with God? And yet the Scriptures are plain in telling us that God wants us to share our lives with Him. So while you are enjoying time spent with your earthly friends, don't forget to be with the greatest Friend you will ever have. You may be separated from earthly friends, but this Friend has promised to never leave or forsake you. Will you start building a stronger relationship with Him today?

Lord, we ask You to grant us a relationship with You that is deeper than ever before. We pray in Jesus's name. Amen.

CHAPTER 24

THE PROBLEM WITH PROBLEMS

T he problem with life is that it is filled with those nasty little creatures that we call "problems." There is probably not a day that goes by that you are not faced with some kind of problem. Problems complicate your life and make it difficult for you to move forward. They are like roadblocks. You are on your way to some important function with little time to spare when suddenly you come to a roadblock or a wreck on the freeway that brings you to a dead stop and forces you to go in a different direction. You can feel your body becoming tense as the stress mounts. You didn't need that complication. You didn't ask for it, but you cannot deny it. It is there, and you have to deal with it.

Problems come in all shapes and sizes with varying degrees of intensity. Some frustrate you and rob you of the peace and joy that you often experience when things are going well. Other problems are much more serious. They not only remove your peace, they threaten you in much deeper ways. For example, the problem of being misunderstood and even rejected by someone you care much about is a loss far greater than simply being detained or slowed down. That kind of rejection hurts, and it hurts deeply. In such cases, you feel the sting of betrayal, and your heart is grieved by the removal of a relationship that leaves a gaping hole in your inner being. Still greater are those problems that have the potential to take away things that we have given our lives to obtain. You may have spent a lifetime building something that you thought to be permanent only to have it suddenly ripped away.

A huge problem raises its ugly head when you or someone you love is diagnosed with a serious health condition. I have a friend who was diagnosed with a progressive, degenerate disease that steadily eats away at his physical abilities. What began small has now grown to the place where he can no longer continue with his previous work schedule. In another situation, a young couple was blessed with a beautiful baby girl. It was not long, however, before doctors discovered some serious birth defects. The intensity of those kinds of problems has the ability to rock your entire world and send you spiraling downward into a pit of despair.

If only your problem would go away, you could take a deep breath of relief and continue onward as you were before the unexpected enemy appeared on the radar screen of your life. You would like to close your eyes and imagine that you are having a bad dream and that you will wake up with the obstacle removed, but reality tells you that is not going to happen. The problem is indeed real, and some way, somehow, you are going to have to face it and deal with it. When you come to such unwanted times, it soon becomes evident that the problem will not be solved by using the conventional wisdom of this world. You need much more than that; you need God. You may not know what to do with a situation that is overwhelmingly powerful in your life, but God has a complete understanding of the total picture. He knows every possible scenario, and He promises to give you wisdom so that you may deal with your problem in the best possible way. James 1:5 says, "If any of you lacks wisdom, he should ask God, who gives generously to all without finding fault, and it will be given to him."

If you choose to follow His wisdom, you will experience the best possible outcome. Having the best possible outcome does not necessarily mean the problem will be solved in the way you would choose. Your understanding is limited at best. His understanding is infinite, and when you respond to your problems according to His plan, everyone will be ultimately blessed. What looks bad will finally be transformed into that which is good. Problems will be turned into opportunities, and He will be faithful to work all things together for the good of those who love Him (see Romans 8:28).

Knowing those truths and even acting on them will not necessarily take away the hurt and the pain of the problem, but it will change the outcome. Whether by all together removing the problem from your life or by removing you from the problem, God's way will always prove itself to be right. It is not ours to understand. It is our place to trust. Even the most damaging problems have a divine answer that will not fail. Place your trust in the unchanging sovereignty of Almighty God who loves you as if you were the only person in the world, and you will find his grace to be sufficient. Second Chronicles 16:9 says, "For the eyes of the LORD range throughout the earth to strengthen those whose hearts are fully committed to him."

In the total scheme of things, our problems will not last forever, but His love for us will. When you cannot understand what He is doing, trust in His love.

Lord, sometimes we are overwhelmed by the problems that seem to regularly flow into our lives, and we don't know what to do about them. So, Lord, our eyes are upon You. Please lead and guide us through the many difficulties we face. We ask this according to Your mercy and grace. We pray in Jesus's name. Amen.

CHAPTER 25

STICKERS

When I was a little boy, summer was not a time when my shoes were used very often. They came out of the closet on Sunday morning for church and then were gladly removed when church was over. The rest of the week, I enjoyed the freedom of running barefoot whether it was on pavement or grass. The pavement sometimes got so hot that I felt like my feet were frying. That is when I would run to someone's yard. Sometimes that worked, but sometimes it didn't. Not everyone had yards of lush, thick grass. Some yards were dry and full of "stickers." When you are running fast over a patch of stickers, you might wish you would have stayed on the pavement. Isn't that like life? You run to get out of a bad situation only to find yourself in another situation that could be even worse.

Where did such things as stickers and the pain they inflict on a little boy's feet come from? They ultimately came from the fall of man. One of the repercussions of the fall and the entrance of sin into this world is that of pain and suffering. Life sometimes hurts, and of all the kinds of pain someone may endure, emotional pain is the worst. Someone may endure physical pain and still be happy, but emotional pain makes life really difficult, and the absence of meaningful relationships and the corresponding loneliness are all "stickers" that pierce your heart. One would only have to quickly review the titles of many of our culture' s songs to see that people are hurting.

When I ran over a sticker patch as a young boy, I didn't see it coming. One minute I was doing great, and then that piercing pain would hit. Neither do you see the stickers that can hold you emotionally captive. You thought the relationship was doing fine, and then you run into the stickers of rejection. You had no idea that person you love was sick. It all happened so fast, and now you are facing the loss of someone dear to your heart. You feel the stickers. Those kinds of things hurt deeply, and you seldom know when you will feel their pain next. Throughout life, there is always the potential of unexpected sticker patches. Friends may forsake you, people may pass away, you may come down with an incurable disease, but in the midst of so much hurt, you can depend on God being there for you. He is the only real constant in your life. All other things and people can be removed from you in a heartbeat.

Moses, the great man of God, wrote Psalm 90. As he trudged his way through the desert, he observed the great mountains that looked as though they had been there forever. In verses 1-2 of this psalm, he said, "Lord, you have been our dwelling place throughout all generations. Before the mountains were born or you brought forth the earth and the world, from everlasting to everlasting you are God."

Yes, those mountains seemed like they had existed eternally. The truth is that only God is eternal, and unlike all other things, you can always count on Him. Stickers happen, and they always will. The positive side is the truth that when you step on stickers, God will always be with you. Psalm 139:7-10 says:

Where can I go from your Spirit? Where can I flee from your presence? If I go up to the heavens, you are there; if I make my bed in the depths, you are there. If I rise on the wings of the dawn, if

I settle on the far side of the sea, even there your hand will guide me, your right hand will hold me fast.

God is always present. He knows all about your pain, and He is ready to help. Oh, the great blessing of having One living within us who completely understands our every need! This is heaven begun below. This is the seed that will one day blossom into full bloom when we reach the eternal state. This is the firstfruits of what will one day be a great emotional harvest when we live in a perfect place with perfect people who are forever blessed by a perfect God. He was with us yesterday. He is with us today, and He will be with us forevermore!

Lord, we thank You so much for loving us and bringing us to Yourself. You have always been present to help us in our time of need. Thank You.

CHAPTER 26

YOUR POTENTIAL

When I was a little kid, I lived in a rural area in northeast Texas. Behind my house was a blackberry patch, a creek filled with tadpoles and little fish, and a trail that would lead you to a small convenience store. I travelled on that small trail regularly with my mind set on a few things to buy. I wanted a Dr Pepper (five cents) and a candy bar (five cents), but the thing I looked forward to most was the latest issue of the *Superman* comic books. I was captivated by this flying man. He was "faster than a speeding bullet, more powerful than a locomotive, and able to leap tall buildings in a single bound." Superman was my man, and I couldn't wait until the newest issue of *Superman* came out. In addition to the comic books, I would be faithful to watch that old black-and-white television version of *Superman* every time it was on. I also liked Batman and Robin, Spider-Man, and the Flash, and I still like that kind of thing.

Superheroes change their world so that it becomes a better place to live. They fight for that which is right, sometimes against great odds. It is clear in the Scriptures that there is a spiritual war going on, and throughout the Bible, you see examples of people that God raised up to bring honor to Him in this battle. The problem is that the average

Christian seems to believe that he doesn't have any real potential to be used by God. Consequently he doesn't get very involved in service for the Lord. We all tend to give too much emphasis to what we can do, and too little emphasis on what God can do.

The book of Judges gives us the example of a young man who seemed thoroughly incapable but whom God used in a great way. The young man's name was Gideon, and by his own admission, he belonged to the weakest tribe in Israel, Manasseh. He belonged to the weakest family of the weakest tribe, and he was the lowest and weakest member of his family. So, to put it all together, Gideon was the lowest and weakest member of the nation! Those are not the kind of credentials that we would normally ask for if we were to interview someone to assume a place of leadership, but God sees things differently than we do. We see Gideon coming on the scene for the first time in Judges 6:11—"The angel of the LORD came and sat down under the oak in Ophrah that belonged to Joash the Abiezrite, where his son Gideon was threshing wheat in a winepress to keep it from the Midianites." Normally a man would thresh wheat on a wooden threshing floor, out in the open in an exposed place, so that the wind could carry away the chaff, but a winepress was carved out of stone and was built down into the ground. It appears that Gideon was afraid that the Midianites would see what he was doing, so he was trying to separate the grain from the chaff down in this cistern below ground level, by walking on it in his bare feet. He was hiding from the enemy. Gideon teaches us some things about the kind of people God uses. God doesn't normally use people who are natural superheroes. He uses unlikely people who are made strong by His power. Your weakness does not hinder God. In fact, 2 Corinthians 12:9 says that His "power is made perfect in weakness."

God loves to show His strength in our weakness. Second Corinthians 3:5 says, "Not that we are competent in ourselves to claim anything for ourselves, but our competence comes from God."

Going back to Gideon, Judges 6:14-16 gives us an interesting dialogue between God and Gideon:

The LORD turned to him and said, "Go in the strength you have and save Israel out of Midian's hand. Am I not sending you?" "But Lord," Gideon asked, "how can I save Israel? My clan is the weakest in Manasseh, and I am the least in my family." The LORD answered, "I will be with you, and you will strike down all the Midianites together."

That statement God made to Gideon—"I will be with you"— explains your own potential for God. You may feel like a Gideon, the least of the least. You may feel like you don't have any special abilities that would benefit the kingdom of God. The truth is that God does not create anyone who does not have the capability to serve Him in some way that will honor Him and bring Him glory. In fact, God can use you greatly if He reduces the abilities that you already consider to be small. That is what He did in the story of Gideon. Gideon's army was greatly outnumbered by the Midianites. Judges 8:10 tells us that the Midianites began the battle with a force of 135,000 men. Meanwhile, Gideon's army consisted of 32,000 men. In other words, Gideon's army was so outnumbered that it was a pretty sure thing that it would be defeated, but that is not the whole story. God later reduced the Israelite army to three hundred men.

Why would God do such a thing? God reduced the already anemic army so that there would be no question in the minds of the Israelites that it was He and He alone who gave the victory. God does not need great numbers to do great things. God needs great people to do great things, people who will live surrendered lives to Him, people who will be filled with the Spirit and who want the glory to be given to Him alone. When you think about how God wants you to serve Him, think big because you have a big God. Jesus said that without Him, we can do nothing (see John 15:5). Paul completed that by saying with Him, we can do all things (see Philippians 4:13). Whenever you feel weak and unable to do what God is calling you to do, remember Gideon. If God can use Gideon, God can certainly use you. Trust Him, leaning upon Him, and step out by faith.

Lord, we are much like Gideon. We are afraid and unsure of ourselves, but we know that Your strength is more than enough for us to be all that You want us to be. Please help us to trust in what You can do through us.
We pray in Jesus's name. Amen.

CHAPTER 27

MAINTAINING GOD-GIVEN RELATIONSHIPS

You never thought it would happen. Someone you were once very close to now seems distant and far removed from your life. As you think back to the time when your relationship with that person was strong, what you feel now is a mixture of hurt, confusion, and even a sense of betrayal. It happens with a close friend whom you often shared the deepest secrets of your heart, things that you would not dare tell anyone else. It happens with an employer who could count on his partner in business to give support and encouragement when things at the company seemed bleak and dismal. It happens to a husband or wife who used to have one heart and one soul. They knew their spouse was the one person they could count on to understand what they were going through. That special gift from God was someone who would not let them down. It happens to a parent who pours his or her life into a child. To Mommy and Daddy, that little child is as dear as life itself, and they willingly abandon many personal dreams in order to meet the needs of that so much loved child, but all of that has changed. The aging parent who gave so much is neglected. In all of these cases and so many more, it seems that loyalty, closeness, and unity of spirit has somehow faded away. What has happened? Why have things so radically changed?

In order to understand why things are the way they are now, you have to understand why things were the way they were before. Why was your soul knit together with that certain person? Such unity of spirit doesn't happen automatically or easily. It comes through doing special things together and through the spending of many hours conversing with one another. It is that kind of devotion to a relationship that is required if you are to have a true "soul mate" or kindred spirit. A truly loving parent will sacrifice much to meet the needs of a loved child. A dating couple will neglect many things if necessary in order to share life with that special somebody. In such cases, it is the relationship that receives priority attention.

If someone is blessed enough to have close, loving relationships with someone, how can such a wonderful thing be lost? Why are things so different than they were before? One major reason for a loss of something that was once so strong is found in the fact of change itself. Change happens. It is a natural occurrence in life, and there is nothing we can do to stop it. The issue is not "if we change." The issue is, "Are we changing together?" The young man goes to college while his wife stays home with their small children. Day after day, his mind is being filled with new thoughts, new dreams, and new perspectives on life. But his wife is not travelling down the same mental road of change. No. She is at home changing diapers, and over time, the two drift apart. Likewise, two friends might be separated over a period of many years. During those years, they live in different environments and are exposed to different ideas. Breathing in those new ideas, they begin to change into different people. The Bible makes it very clear that we are what we think: "For as he thinks within himself, so he is" (Proverbs 23:7 NASB).

If those two close friends change independently of one another for long enough, they will have little, if anything, in common. All that will remain is a vague memory of what once was many years ago. Changing together is essential if two people are to retain intimacy with one another. Those two people must spend time talking, discussing, and even sometimes debating, all of which mold the two lives together so that intimacy remains solid and firm. Failure to spend the time necessary to change together is to guarantee that what you thought would never happen will happen. Friends will no longer know one another. Family members will be estranged from one another, and even children and parents will no longer enjoy the closeness of family that God intends to be. What is it worth to maintain a relationship that was once so special? Ask yourself the question, "Is this a relationship that God wants to remain close? Is this something that the Scriptures encourage or even command?" God gives us good gifts. In fact, the Bible says that "every good gift and perfect gift is from above . . ." (James 1:17).

What good relationships has God given you in the past that are now in a state of deterioration? Never count lightly what God counts seriously. Instead do your part by injecting new energy into the floundering relationship, and ask God to restore what has been lost. Doing so will cost, but no matter how costly obeying God may seem, the blessing of God will always far outweigh the burden.

Lord, spare us from our own selfishness and help us in our relationships. Amen.

CHAPTER 28

DISAPPOINTED EXPECTATIONS

One of my greatest desires as I was growing up was to have a motorcycle. I mean, I really, really wanted a motorcycle. If I never received another birthday present or another Christmas present, that would have been fine with me if I could only have a motorcycle. That didn't happen, because my parents were firmly against it, and they would not budge. They would just as soon have me sleeping at night with a rattlesnake in my bed as to have a motorcycle. At the time, I felt their decision to be unfair. Other boys had motorcycles, and I did not see them getting hurt. So why was I denied my greatest heart's desire?

If you won't tell anyone, I'll let you know a little secret. The secret is that, although more decades than I would like to mention have passed by, I would still like to have a motorcycle. You might ask, "Then why don't you get one?" When I was younger, I had parents who would not let me have a motorcycle. Now that I am older, my wife doesn't want me to have one. What kind of deal is that! I wanted. I wanted. Oh, how I wanted a motorcycle! But time and time again, my expectations were dashed against the rocks.

Disappointed expectations hurt. The young boy works hard to make the team, but he is not chosen. The young lady diligently studies in hopes of making a score that will be high enough to gain acceptance into the college of her choice, but she fails.

Everyone sees his expectations come to nothing at some time or another, but the problem is made much more complex if one happens to be a Christian. That is because Christians are told that there is a God in heaven who cares for us, who has all power, and who can do all things. He has told us that if we ask, we will receive. He invites us to pray, and He has promised to answer our prayers. So in obedience to Him, we strive to believe His Word and His promises, and we expect our God to answer.

When He doesn't answer our sincere cries, we are confused and are often thrust into a crisis of faith. We just don't understand why God would not answer our prayers. Has God forgotten his promise, or is there some kind of hidden sin within our hearts? Is God punishing us for something that we have done? Is He really even there?

The answer is simple. Sometimes the things we think would be a blessing would really be a curse to us (like a motorcycle for a certain young boy). Going back to the days of my youth, I now realize that given the nature and temperament that I had, the chances of me being hurt badly or killed were far greater than the chance that I would have not been injured.

The fact is that if we were to see the end result of some of our prayers being answered, we would not like what we see. Sometimes if we got what we want, we wouldn't want what we got. The Scriptures say that God will withhold "no good thing" from us (Psalm 84:11). Thank God, He knows what is good for us and what is bad for us. The next time you are tempted to question the faithfulness of God, remember that motorcycles are not good for everyone. Although my parents' decision seemed at the time to be unwarranted and uncaring, today I see it as being one of wisdom and protection. In fact, I believe that God worked through my parents to protect me from what would probably have been a catastrophe. Sometimes our greatest desires would do us the greatest harm if God gave them to us. When we don't understand His actions, we can remember His loving heart. His understanding has no limit, and His love is so great that He is willing to be misunderstood in order to protect us from things that would hurt us. Praise Him when He answers with a "Yes," and trust Him when He answers with a "No," because whether "Yes" or "No," the answer is a perfect one that proceeds from a mind of infinite intelligence and a heart of absolute love.

Lord, we don't always know what is best for us. Thank You for sometimes saying
"No" to those things that would damage us. Help us to not
fret but rather to trust.

CHAPTER 29

MAKING HARD DECISIONS

We are all acquainted with decisions. Decision-making is as much a part of life as breathing, but every once in a while, we are called upon to make a decision that is exceptionally hard. I experienced such a decision one year when our family returned from a two-week vacation. While we were away, our family dog, named "Bear," became sick with something that seemed to be parasitic. My son and I took him to the veterinarian, who informed us that the treatment to keep Bear alive would be expensive, and that there were no guarantees that he would live.

You may have heard the expression "poor as Job's turkey." That was certainly our condition at the time, especially after a two-week vacation. I knew there was only so far that I could go financially, and the price of the treatment was over the top. It was decision time. With no guarantees of Bear's survival and no money, I decided that we must say good-bye to our dear friend Bear. How do you decide something like that when your son is standing beside you looking at his beloved dog and wanting with all that is within him to take his dog home? Those are decisions you wish you would never have to make. If you could wake up to find that this is only a bad dream, you would be very relieved. But the decision is not a dream.

Bear was in a cage looking straight at us as if to say, "Are you going to take me home now? When we get home, can we go jogging? Please take me out of this cage." Bear wanted to go home with his family, and I was telling the technician to end his life. My brokenhearted son walked over to Bear's cage and said a few simple words that brought tears to the eyes of the technician, words I will never forget as long as I live. Realizing what was about to take place, my son said, "Good-bye, Bear. I love you." With that, we turned and walked out of the building, forever leaving our friend Bear.

Life is filled with soul-wrenching times like that. You or someone in your family may be in poor health, and you must decide if surgery is the option to take. You may be in a relationship with someone who you don't think is right for you, and you have to make the decision to end it. Whatever your hard decision is, it is looking you straight in the face, and you must answer either "Yes" or "No."

Normally speaking, children are shielded from such devastating choices because they have the luxury of having a mom or dad who can make the hard decisions for them. It is a blessing to remember that no matter how old you are, you still have a heavenly Father who is more concerned about your life than you are. He loves you, and He wants the best for your life. In fact, Romans 12:2 says that God's will is "good, pleasing and perfect." The key to that verse is the one that precedes it. Romans 12:1 tells us to present our bodies as a living sacrifice. Knowing God's will is not a formula. It is a relationship. When we live surrendered to God, we find our will blending with His will, and His desires becoming our desires. Drawing near to God is vital if you are to hear His voice clearly and receive His direction.

Proverbs 16:3 says, "Commit to the LORD whatever you do, and your plans will succeed." The words "Commit to the LORD whatever you do" are a key element in the whole process. Clarity comes as you surrender your will and your way to the Lord. It is then that your plans will succeed.

It may be that as you are reading this devotional, you are going through a very difficult time and have some hard decisions to make. It may be that you feel like running away, and the destination is really not important. You just don't want to have to deal with what you are facing. The good news is that you don't have to be stressed out and frightened, because God promises to guide you.

Some of the issues you face will never be understood, at least in this lifetime. Why did God allow our family dog Bear to die and leave us when we loved him? I don't know the answer to that question, but the passing of years has taught me that God always has a reason for what He allows. There was a reason that God allowed Abraham to wait so long for the son He had promised. There was a reason Moses had to spend forty years of his life taking care of sheep, and there is a reason for the trial that you are presently facing. To understand that your predicament is not the result of random chance, but rather something God intends to bring good out of, is the key to being strong enough to make that hard decision that is crushing your spirit. If you really believe that God wants to guide you, you can face your decision with confidence as you rest in His everlasting arms. As Peter said, you can "Cast all your anxiety on him because he cares for you" (1 Peter 5:7).

Lord, sometimes we would do anything rather than make the hard decisions that stare us in the face. We are threatened and sometimes sad or confused. Please help us to have a faith in You that will give us peace. We pray in Jesus's name. Amen.

CHAPTER 30

YOUR ATTENTION PLEASE

Any public speaker knows the importance of getting and keeping the attention of his audience. If he fails in that one point, he will not succeed in communicating his message. You may have heard a parent telling his child to "pay attention" to what he or she is saying. The problem is sometimes we just don't listen until something happens that gets our attention.

There is an illustration from 2 Samuel 14 that illustrates that truth. According to the story, King David's son Absalom was calling for the commander of the army, Joab, to come to him. Second Samuel 14:28-31 says:

Then Absalom sent for Joab in order to send him to the king, but Joab refused to come to him. So he sent a second time, but he refused to come. Then he said to his servants, "Look, Joab's field is next to mine, and he has barley there. Go and set it on fire." So Absalom's servants set the field on fire. Then Joab did go to Absalom's house, and he said to him, "Why have your servants set my field on fire?"

Sometimes God is calling to us to come to Him, but we are paying him no attention—no attention, that is, until He begins burning our "barley fields." I remember an incident from my childhood that is similar to this story.

One hot summer day, my younger brother, Gerald, went out on the back patio when the grass was dry and crisp. He carried with him a play rifle designed to shoot out a cork, but Gerald had a better idea. Instead of using the rifle to shoot a cork, he put a firecracker in the gun, lit the firecracker, and shot it out into the yard. So what do you think happened as a result of his expert marksmanship? Probably what you would expect: the backyard caught on fire.

When Gerald saw the work of his hands, he ran into the house to find my mother, and he found her in a locked bathroom where she was dyeing her eyebrows. Frantically he cried out, "Mother!" But before he could finish, my mother cut him off and said, "Gerald, don't bother me now. I'm busy dyeing my eyebrows."

Gerald again said, "Mother!" but once more, he was cut off.

"Gerald, I told you not to bother me!"

"But mother!" Gerald said.

By this time, our mother was getting quite disturbed with my little brother and cautioned him to not bother her again. That's when Gerald blurted out, "The backyard is on fire!"

Never have you seen a door open as quickly as my mother opened the bathroom door. She dashed through the den and out into a backyard that was quickly being devoured by the flames. Soon a huge red fire truck rushed to our home and took down our fence so that they could get to the fire. That was when an older brother should give a younger brother sound advice, and I did not fail in doing so: "You'd better get out of here while you have time."

I wonder how often God is calling us to do something, but we are not listening. We would never say it, but inwardly we, like my mother, are saying, "God, don't bother me now. I'm doing something extremely important." If God calls again, we give the same answer. Then, like the two stories above, God gets our attention. When He does, suddenly things that seemed to be so important don't seem important anymore.

What has God used to get your attention? God's method of getting our attention is as different as there are numbers of people. What would get me up and running toward God and His will may not have the same effect on you. Carefully, God selects the exact tool that He knows will be most effective for each one of us. The loss of a job, a prolonged sickness, or the ending of a relationship that we put before Him are only some of the ways God may direct our focus to Him.

We have probably all gone through this process many times, but we are slow learners. When God burns our barley fields, He does it for our good. Hebrews 12:10-11 says:

Our fathers disciplined us for a little while as they thought best; but God disciplines us for our good, that we may share in his holiness. No discipline seems pleasant at the time, but painful. Later on, however, it produces a harvest of righteousness and peace for those who have been trained by it.

When God deals with us, it is not fun, but it is profitable. Scripture says His intention is to produce a "harvest of righteousness and peace." Whether we become bitter or better by the experience is determined by our response. We can hang onto our toys, or we can let go and receive his treasure. Always remember that God does not call us unless there is a reason, and that reason eventually turns to our blessing. Rather than being like Joab, God wants us to be like Jesus. Hebrews 12:2 says, "Let us fix our eyes on Jesus, the author and perfecter of our faith, who for the joy set before him endured the cross, scorning its shame, and sat down at the right hand of the throne of God." When God the Father called, the Lord Jesus answered, and so should we. Don't wait until you smell smoke before you come to God.

Father, with our minds, we believe You know what is best. Help our hearts to catch up with our minds, and help us to listen to You and obey You. We pray this in Jesus's name.

CHAPTER 31

THE GIFT OF MEMORY

Some things speak for themselves. The warm embrace of two friends needs no interpretation. The unsolicited hug from one spouse to the other is understood in any language. So it is with the giving of gifts. When someone gives us a gift, that gift is a token of his friendship or love for us. While we appreciate the gifts people give us, we must remember that God is the greatest Giver. In fact, James 1:17 tells us "Every good and perfect gift is from above." James says all good gifts ultimately come from the hand of God. If we were to take the time, we could write a long list of the good gifts God has given. What would be on your list? In all probability, you would list such things as your family, your job, your home, and your health. All of those things are to be greatly appreciated, but have you ever thought about the gift of memory?

The gift of memory is a wonderful thing. It allows us to think our way into the past and to mentally relive events that took place long, long ago. I remember vaguely my grandfather bringing me a little black puppy when I was five years old. I remember Christmas gifts, such as a little wooden rifle, a red-and-white record player, and a little fox terrier that I named "Sugar." In giving us the gift of memory, God has given to us something that plants, animals, and machines do not possess in the way that we do.

Dogs have memories, but I doubt very seriously that a grown dog has vivid memories of what it was like being a puppy. Of all the creatures God has made, we alone have the ability to think back into the past and to make logical and detailed future decisions based upon what we remember.

Using the gift of memory in the right way is important to God. In Deuteronomy 8:2, Moses told the generation that was to enter the Promised Land the following words: "Remember how the LORD your God led you all the way in the desert these forty years, to humble you and to test you in order to know what was in your heart." As that generation finally prepared to enter the land, Joshua told one man from each tribe to help make a pile of stones in the River Jordan as a remembrance. Then Joshua said, "In the future, when your children ask you, 'What do these stones mean?' tell them that the flow of the Jordan was cut off before the ark of the covenant of the LORD. When it crossed the Jordan, the waters of the Jordan were cut off" (Joshua 4:6-7). Clearly God wants us to remember the good things that He has done throughout our lives.

Do you ever spend time reminiscing about what it was like when you first came to know the Lord? Those early days of spiritual childhood should serve as an encouragement that rekindles the spiritual flame in our hearts and motivates us to go on to maturity. Future trials lose their power as we think of God's faithfulness in previous trials. We need to remember how God has led us through our own spiritual deserts and how He has many times parted our Jordan Rivers. We need to erect spiritual stones in our minds that mark times when God did special things for us.

We never grow out of the need to remember. The apostle Peter said to his readers, "So I will always remind you of these things, even though you know them and are firmly established in the truth you now have" (2 Peter 1:12). No matter how firmly rooted you are in the Scriptures, you need to purposely remind yourself of even the most basic spiritual truths. Peter goes on to say in verse 13, "I think it is right to refresh your memory . . . ." Often we are so caught up in life's trials and hardships that we tend to forget the great things God has done for us. We need to refocus and remember so that we can be refreshed.

On the other hand, not all memories are positive. For some, remembering the past is a disturbing thing that keeps them locked in an emotional prison. Many remember being the object of parental neglect. They are haunted by the partiality shown to other siblings and still feel angry and insecure. Some people are plagued with memories of times when they did things that were destructive to their well-being. Memory is a powerful thing. It can lift us up and help us in our journey of faith, and it has the ability to plunge us into the depths of despair. One of the encouraging things about memory is that it is selective. You don't have to dwell on the negative things that have hurt you in the past. You can choose to remember the good rather than the bad. The reason some people have a never-ending well of praise is that they are choosing to draw from the well of uplifting, edifying experiences.

How are you using God's gift of memory? Do you allow memories of a tainted past to freely flow into your mind, or do you guard your heart and choose to think about those things that will build strength into your life? God has given you a gift. It is your choice as to how it will be used. It can become your best friend, or it can become a stumbling block that prevents you from becoming all that God intends for you to be.

God, You have told us in Your Word to set our minds on heavenly things. Help us to be filled with Your Word so that our lives may be lived by its laws. Amen.

CHAPTER 32

THE JOY OF FAMILY LIFE

One day many years ago, my father was having a birthday. I don't know what inspired me, but I decided that I would make him a birthday cake. This was not going to be just any cake. This was going to be an extraordinary cake that people would talk about for years to come. I checked the recipe book and gathered all the ingredients needed to create an incredible birthday cake. As I looked at the recipe, I decided that I would go above and beyond what was called for in the recipe.

For example, the recipe called for a certain amount of eggs to be mixed in with the flour, but I thought that more would mean better. Excitedly, I imagined how much better this cake was going to taste with those extra eggs. I mixed in the food coloring, stirred all the ingredients together, and then put this soon-to-be-famous cake batter in the oven. I went out of the room while the cake was baking—only to find something far different than I had expected upon my return. There was a blue stream of batter flowing out of the inside of the oven and onto the outside. It flowed down the oven to the cabinets, and probably found its resting place on the floor. The extra eggs had caused the problem.

The moral of the story is that if you want to receive God's "cakes," you follow His "recipe." That is true in every walk of life. Galatians 6:7 says, "Do not be deceived: God cannot be mocked. A man reaps what he sows." We understand this principle in most situations in life. If we want to become a teacher, we must sow seeds of much study. If we want to become a great athlete, we must sow seeds of many hard hours of practice. In the same way, if we want to have a good family life, we also must sow the right kind of seeds.

Family life is meant by God to be a great blessing to our lives. I have lived long enough, been through enough, and seen enough to know that the things many people are striving so hard to obtain do not bring lasting happiness, but the right kind of family does. When I was growing up, I had the privilege of being a part of a large extended family with many aunts, uncles, and cousins. I also had two grandmothers and two great aunts. Unusual to our society today, they all lived in the same town with a population being around five hundred people. That meant they all lived very close together and regularly shared meals and visited with one another in their homes.

The thing that made this special was the bond of love that existed between those people. Being a part of that closely knit group of relatives provided a sense of stability, significance, and of security, and when we were together, we were happy and blessed.

When I grew up, I married my wife Beth, and we were blessed with two children of our own, one boy and one girl. Now those days have come and gone, but the memories of our family life remain embedded forever in my heart. I remember taking my son and playing miniature golf and then getting an ice cream cone. I remember a certain night of the week when I would take my daughter on what we called "cookie night." On that particular night, we would go to a health-food store, buy a package of cookies, and then take them to the car where we would eat every last one of them. Thanksgiving was a special time for my son and me as we had our annual Thanksgiving bicycle ride. I remember taking a short vacation with my wife and walking on the river walk in San Antonio. All of those times were happy times because God intends the family to be a blessing. The problem is you don't get the blessing unless you follow the recipe, and our contemporary society has radically changed the recipe from God's to a secular approach to life.

We are told that the way to happiness is to make a lot of money and have many things. Nothing could be further from the truth. You may enjoy your new big-screen television with all the latest bells and whistles, but it will not give you the security of knowing that someone loves you. Driving a new car maybe fun, but it cannot take you to the place of permanent happiness. Only God can do that. Our society needs strong fathers who will lead their families in the ways of the Lord. In Genesis 18:19, God said of Abraham, "For I have chosen him, so that he will direct his children and his household after him to keep the way of the LORD by doing what is right and just, so that the LORD will bring about for Abraham what he has promised him." Then, in Joshua 24:15, Joshua said, "as for me and my household, we will serve the LORD." Our families also need strong mothers like the lady who is described in Proverbs 31.

Families are a blessing if they follow God's recipe. How about you and your family? Are you diligently following the recipe of the Word of God in your family life? Don't miss the blessing by substituting the things this world has to offer. Give your family your best, and you in turn will receive the best.

Father in heaven, our world confuses us with principles that are not in line with Your Word. Help us to be strong enough to go against the flow of our society by raising up godly families for Your glory and for our good. We pray in Jesus's name. Amen.

CHAPTER 33

WILL YOU FINISH THE RACE?

When I was a much younger man, I was an avid jogger. As soon as I woke up and exited my bed, the jogging shoes went on, and I was out the door. Sometimes I jogged on a track at one of the local schools, and at other times, I burned up the pavement in my neighborhood. Wherever the jogging took place, it was always driven by a desire to go farther or faster or both. Improvement was the name of the game.

That kind of enthusiasm and dedication was much like what happens in someone's life when he becomes a Christian. When the young Christian wakes up in the morning, it is the Christian race that is on his mind. Just as I wanted to go farther in my jogging, the young Christian has a sincere desire to learn more about his newfound faith. He wants to go further with God than he has ever gone before, and he wants to do it as quickly as possible.

Becoming a new jogger or a new Christian can be an exciting thing that fills one with hopes and dreams of things yet to come. Unfortunately, as the days turn into weeks and the weeks become months, the enthusiasm sometimes begins to wane, and it becomes easier to replace a morning jog with some extra time in the sack. In much the same way, the Christian can easily find other things more alluring than Bible study and prayer.

Sometimes we experience another curious problem. Somehow, someway, a small rock, a pebble has found its way into our shoes, and our jog becomes uncomfortable. We pick up physical pebbles off the street, and spiritual "pebbles" are the result of some sin in our life that is not yet surrendered to God. Sometimes people let pebbles accumulate in their shoes to the point that they stop the race altogether. I also have been around long enough to see some good spiritual runners fall away from God. I am reminded of Galatians 5:7 (ESV) in those instances: "You were running well. Who hindered you from obeying the truth?" The problem is usually not the big things in our lives that derail us and take us out of the race. The problem is those little pebbles that have accumulated over a period of time. Having started out running the Christian race with all of our might, we find ourselves limping along. That's when we lose our joy and begin going through a tiring routine that has no future.

It would be unrealistic for us to think that we will not pick up some pebbles in our spiritual shoes as we run the course of life. It would be just as unrealistic to think that we can continue with those pebbles. If we do not do something to remove them, we will eventually stop the race and fail to accomplish God's purpose for our lives. We must be careful to clean out our shoes every day. That is what 1 John 1:9 is all about. God says that if we agree with him concerning our sin, then He is faithful to forgive us and to cleanse us from all unrighteousness. So keep your heart clean and run the race for God. When you cross your finish line, you will be glad you did.

Lord, You have given each of us a race to run. Help us to run in such a way that You will be glorified. Amen.

CHAPTER 34

BE CAREFUL

If you are reading this book, it is probably because you want to be closer to the Lord and serve Him more faithfully. Perhaps you did not grow up in a Christian home with godly parents who taught you God's ways. Instead you were taught the ways of the world, and you embraced them wholeheartedly. Yours was a dramatic conversion experience that surprised those who knew you. Some were skeptical that you would continue, but you have continued and have blessed many by your example. Your progress in your walk with God is a wake-up call for those who do not know Christ. They see before their very eyes the transformation of a life that screams loudly that God is real and convicts them of their spiritual need. Sadly some do not continue in their spiritual growth. That is not a new thing. It is as old as Christianity itself. As we saw in the last chapter, Paul said to the churches in Galatia: "You were running well. Who hindered you from obeying the truth?" (Galatians 5:7 ESV).

I have seen church members fervently involved in God's work, only to see them slowly drift away. I have seen friends encourage me and serve God beside me, but they now no longer serve God. Without question, that is an extremely hard experience. To feel so close to someone, to depend on their encouragement and then to wake up one morning to find that it is all gone is a tragedy. The question is very simply, "Why?" Why would someone who started out with a heart of enthusiasm, someone who openly proclaimed his or her their faith and stood against the evil in our world, switch sides and become a part of the problem rather than the solution? It may appear that the erring sheep just suddenly without any warning left the fold. The truth is, however, that the slide downward starts inwardly long before we see its expression outwardly. There has been, unaware to us, a gradual decline in that person's heart for some time before it is obvious in his or her outward behavior.

Hebrews 2:1 says, "We must pay more careful attention, therefore, to what we have heard, so that we do not drift away." Notice that the author of Hebrews likened the decline in spirituality to drifting. Many years ago when I was only around fourteen years of age, I went fishing with my father on a huge lake. I remember that when we reached certain places in the water, he would cut the motor off and fish from that particular location for a while. The problem was that if the boat was not securely tied to some immovable object, such as a strong shrub, it would drift. It was surprising to see how far away the boat could drift in a short amount of time. It drifted so far that my dad would have to crank the boat's motor and go back to where he was before the drift began. The same thing happens to us spiritually. Sometimes we drift away from the Lord. While fishing that day, drifting in our boat made us unable to be successful in catching fish. When the boat of our lives drifts, we can no longer grow stronger in the Lord. Instead we either stagnate or drift into dangerous waters. The drift happens so slowly that we do not even recognize that we are moving. When reading and meditating on the Scriptures becomes a chore, we are drifting. When we no longer spend as much time in prayer, or when prayer loses its passion and becomes a religious routine, we are drifting. When we lose sight of the eternal realities we once held so dear and place our affection on the things of this world, we are drifting.

The answer is to commit ourselves to living an uncompromising life. The prophet Daniel is an example to us of how to persevere in righteous living. From his earliest days, Daniel refused to compromise. As a young person, he refused to eat to meat from the king's table (see Daniel 1:8-16). When it was late in his life, he refused to stop praying to the true God (see Daniel 6). Daniel lived a life of uncompromising integrity.

Living such a life of uncompromising integrity earned Daniel respect from godly people, but most of all, it pleased God. We must dare to be a Daniel and go against the flow. We must be willing to say "No" when everyone else is saying "Yes," when in fact we would even like to say "Yes." We must refuse to give an inch that would later turn into a mile. If everyone throughout the history of this world who has compromised their values were to be able to speak to you, they would all tell you the same thing: it is not worth it. Why would we give up God's best and trade it for a mediocre Christian life that impacts and changes no one, including ourselves?

Hebrews 12:1-2 says, ". . . and let us run with perseverance the race marked out for us. Let us fix our eyes on Jesus, the author and perfecter of faith, who for the joy set before him endured the cross, scorning its shame, and sat down at the right hand of the throne of God." Jesus Christ knew what it was to suffer because He would not accept the standards of his world, but He also knew the joy of fulfilling the Father's will. What about you? Are you as fervent about God today as you were one year ago? Beware of the danger of drifting. It will take you where you never thought you would go, and it will rob you of the best the God has for your life.

Lord, You are our only hope. Protect us from compromise and help us to live a holy life. In Jesus's name. Amen.

CHAPTER 35

SICKNESS

A mong the many problems people face, sickness is particularly dreaded. There are thousands of ways that you can experience sickness. Anything from a mild cold that is no more than a nuisance to terminal heart failure is all referred as "sickness." Sickness can slow us down, and it has the power to stop us altogether. We know one thing for sure, whether it is a runny nose or a failing heart, we don't want it. God joins us in our dislike for sickness because sickness was not in His original plan His created people. Sickness is a part of the curse that began plaguing people after man sinned in the Garden of Eden.

Our biggest concern, however, is not the history of sickness. Our greatest concern is how to get rid of it. We thank God for gifted doctors who can help us when we are ill, but somehow we cry out for something more. We find our eyes looking upward to a greater source of power. We say with the psalm writer in Psalm 121:1-3, "I lift up my eyes to the hills—where does my help come from? My help comes from the LORD, the Maker of heaven and earth."

Doctors are to be respected for what they do, but they are all limited. So our hearts call out to the One who knows no limit. We must never forget that God can heal people, even people who are pronounced terminal.

When I was about seven months old, I became very ill. The diagnosis was not good. I had pneumonia in both lungs, and I continued to decline in health. One night, my grandmother, who was a loving, nurturing person, suddenly became commander in chief. She was adamant that I had to go to the hospital and that it had to be that night. Since there was no hospital in the little town we lived in, we were off to Shreveport, Louisiana. It was indeed a dire situation, and by the time of arrival, I could hardly breathe. I was turning blue, and a Catholic nun gave me last rites. Then I was taken to the doctor, who exclaimed, "Why have they brought a dead baby for me to operate on?"

In what was probably considered a vain attempt, a tracheotomy was performed on a child who had very little chance of making it. At least that's the way it appeared on a human level. The truth is, however, that there is more to life than what we perceive with our five senses. As the prophet Daniel once said to Nebuchadnezzar, ". . . there is a God in heaven . . ." (Daniel 2:28), and unknown to the doctors, there was a church in that small town that had an all-night prayer meeting for me. And you know what happened? Miraculously, I made it.

Would I have made it apart from the prayer meeting? All indications say "No." I am alive and able to write these words because God answers prayer. James 5:17 tells us: "Elijah was a man just like us. He prayed earnestly that it would not rain, and it did not rain on the land for three and a half years. Again he prayed, and the heavens gave rain, and the earth produced its crops." When the doctors have done all they know to do, it is still not over until the Great Physician makes that decision. We, as twenty-first-century Christians need a wake-up call in this matter of healing. So often, our prayer that someone will be healed is weak and anemic.

Prayer becomes no more than a spiritual "rabbit's foot." We don't expect God to heal, but it won't hurt to try. The reality is that the

113

Limitless One, the One who spoke the world into existence and flung the stars into space has plenty of power to do anything He desires. The nagging question is, "Why does God heal some people but not others?"

Is it because some people don't have enough faith? That may sometimes be true, but it is far from being the only answer. There is no magical formula to follow that brings God's healing. In the Bible, Jesus sometimes healed people because they had faith. He also healed other people because someone else with faith prayed for them. Sometimes He initiated the healing, and sometimes sick people came to Him. We must be reminded that God is sovereign and cannot be put in a box of our making.

Why would God not heal some people? As far as it is from our thinking, God knows that some people need a "thorn in the flesh" so that they will draw near to him with greater dependence than they would if they were healed. Paul's thorn in the flesh kept him from being proud (see 2 Corinthians 12:7-10). I suspect that the same is true for many of us. God also places all of us in divinely chosen circumstances that we may be a witness to people like family members, fellow workers, and neighbors, so that we can be living demonstrations of His power. When they see us going through negative circumstances, perhaps prolonged illnesses or the loss of a job with a joy in our heart and a smile on our face, it becomes difficult to deny the fact that there is something more to our lives than what meets the eye. They are compelled to believe that we are operating in a strength that is greater than what can be found in our own humanness.

Nothing could be any more powerful a witness than that kind of undeniable strength. So cheer up, suffering believer. It may seem as though your sick body is keeping you from your full potential when in reality it is causing you to reach your full potential. Yes, there will come a time when the suffering will be over, maybe in six months, a year, five years, or maybe not until eternity, but it will be over. Until that time, take heart as you remember Romans 8:18, which says, "I consider that our present sufferings are not worth comparing with the glory that will be revealed in us."

Dear heavenly Father, our suffering is hard, and we would like for You to remove it from us, but even more than that, we want to give You glory. We thank You that You can take the weak things of life and use them to strongly impact those who watch Your mighty power at work within our lives. We ask You to give us the faith to receive Your healing, and the faith to go on with Your joy if You choose not to heal on this side of heaven. Most of all, continue Your work in us until our earthly course is finished. We thank You
in Jesus's name. Amen.

CHAPTER 36

THE SEEING OF FAITH

By faith Moses, when he had grown up, refused to be known as the son of Pharaoh's daughter. He chose to be mistreated along with the people of God rather than to enjoy the pleasures of sin for a short time. He regarded disgrace for the sake of Christ as of greater value than the treasures of Egypt, because he was looking ahead to his reward. By faith he left Egypt, not fearing the king's anger; he persevered because he saw him who is invisible. (Hebrews 11:24-27)

There is no question that Moses was one of the greatest characters in the Bible. What a man this Moses was! As a child, he was taken out of the water by Pharaoh's daughter and then became the prince of Egypt. During those first forty years of his life, Moses appeared to be powerful. As a potential future king, he received the best education possible in his day. In addition, he learned the military strategies of Egypt and was trained to be a great leader. Anyone observing Moses at that stage of his life would have thought that he had risen to the pinnacle of success. He was the epitome of all that was considered great in the eyes of his contemporaries.

The Scriptures, however, tell us that God doesn't see things as we do. With God, it is the inside—the heart—that counts. If someone doesn't have a heart that is yielded to God, if someone doesn't have a passion for God's glory, nothing else really matters. Moses had received his education in Egypt, but there came a time when God was ready for him to enroll in the divine university: the desert. After being raised in the palace, he appeared to be powerful. After he graduated from the desert, he would actually be powerful. Power with God does not come from a strong arm. It comes from a submissive spirit. It took forty long years working in the hot desert to teach Moses the kind of humility that all of God's warriors must possess. Moses's graduation ceremony came from a burning bush. It was there that Moses received his marching orders to do what he had been prepared for eighty years to do.

Truly the hard times, the lonely hours, and the humiliation of being a common shepherd had transformed this man into a powerful vessel for God to use. Can you imagine marching into Egypt and confronting Pharaoh, the most powerful man on the face of the earth, demanding that he let his work force go free? Can you imagine being in charge of millions of uncooperative, complaining people, and taking them through a vast, uncharted desert? Then think of standing at an impassable Red Sea with screaming, frantic people all around you and the armies of Pharaoh getting closer by the minute. And then, with the strength that was characteristic of his walk with God, holding up his rod and, with confidence, saying, "stand firm, and see the salvation of the LORD" (Exodus 14:13 ESV). What a man this Moses was! The key to Moses's strength is seen in Hebrews 11:27, which tells us that Moses "persevered because he saw him who is invisible." Moses saw the invisible God with the seeing that comes through faith.

Faith is a sort of sixth sense that God gives to His people. True faith sometimes leads us to do things that seem strange and unusual.

For example, Hebrews 11:25 tells us that Moses chose mistreatment with the people of God over the enjoyment of this world. Verse 26 tells us that he chose disgrace over the treasures of Egypt. That would make no sense at all unless Moses saw something that others did not and could not see, and he did—by faith. By faith, the curtain that separates the seen world from the unseen world was opened so that Moses was able to see things that are far more valuable than the things on the visible side of the curtain. It was this seeing by faith that made Moses the great man that we know. Moses was strong because Moses knew God. That's it. That's the bottom line. Today Moses stands as an example of what God can do in the life of someone who makes decisions based upon unseen spiritual realities. It is when we see Him who is invisible that we're able to do the impossible by the strength of an almighty God who works on our behalf. He is still doing miracles. He is there for your Red Sea crossings. He is there when the burden seems unbearable, and He is there to lead you through your wilderness. Do you see Him who is invisible?

Lord, help us to see by faith what we can't see by sight. Help us to believe when we don't see and to obey even when doing so doesn't seem like the best thing. Help us to believe that You will act when everyone around us says You won't. Amen.

CHAPTER 37

RUNNING OUT OF STEAM

When I was about twelve years old, I used to go to the local YMCA. It was there that I learned to play ping-pong along with a lot of other fun games. On one particular day, I was walking along the sidewalk with some friends when we saw a lot of people gathered at the end of the building. Naturally we were curious and wanted to know what was happening, so we made our way down to the crowd. It didn't take long for us to understand what was creating the excitement. It was a race that was about to begin any moment. I don't have any idea why, but my friends were urging me to run in the race. It was not because I was a runner. I had never even thought of participating in a race. Nevertheless, after much persuasion from my buddies, I became a contender.

When the race started, I jumped ahead of the pack, and my friends were loving it. Everything was going great until the race was almost over. It was at that point that I heard a disturbing sound. My lead was narrowing, and the ominous sound was that of the other boys coming up behind me. Then it happened. One by one, boys passed me by as my friends screamed at me to run faster, but to no avail. My legs felt like they were numb, and they refused to obey what my mind was telling them to do. Let me jump to the end. I lost the race because I ran out of steam.

Does that sound familiar to you? It certainly does to me because, to be honest with you, many times I feel like I'm running out of steam. Physically I am exhausted. Emotionally I am on "empty," and the "peace of God, which transcends all understanding" (Philippians 4:7) is ebbing away in the spiritual realm of life. It's not that I don't want to run faster. It is simply that my spiritual legs are numb, and sometimes everything within me wants to quit. That is not a good condition to be in, and when we are told in the Scriptures to rejoice always in any and every situation, then obviously something has not worked according to plan.

As a boy in that race long ago, I made a number of mistakes. First, I did not train for the race. I suppose I thought that I could win without preparing to win. I was wrong! Preparation is essential if we are to win in any worthwhile endeavor.

The Christian life is not any different. The Scriptures are clear that spiritual success does not accidentally fall into our laps. In 1 Corinthians 9:24, Paul said, "Do you not know that in a race all the runners run, but only one gets the prize? Run in such a way as to get the prize." Spiritual victory comes only to those who want it bad enough to prepare for it. If we are to win, we must spend time each day taking in nourishment from the Word of God and by spending time in the presence of the Holy One. It is there in the secret place that we prepare for the game of life, and without that preparation, it is impossible for us to win.

Another mistake that I made in my first and last race was failing to pace myself. The boys behind me were not behind because they could not run any faster. They were purposely pacing themselves so they would have ample strength to not only run, but to finish the race well. We are not machines that can continually go on and on. We are human beings who only have a limited amount of energy in our lives. If we pour it all out on the front end of life, we will find out sooner or later that we don't have anything left as we approach the end. Life is not a sprint. It is a marathon, and marathon runners must save some of their energy for the last part of the race. If they don't, they will lose the competition.

Your willpower will not get you across the finish line. Only the grace of God can do that. If we would spend more time being concerned about being filled with God's grace than we are about how busy we can be, we will go a lot further in our goal to win the race of life.

Lord, help us to look to You and Your power as we run the race of life.
This we pray in Jesus's name. Amen.

CHAPTER 38

WHAT DO YOU SEE?

How is your vision? Are you able to see clearly? As I was growing up, I never had anything but perfect vision, and I never imagined that it would be any different, but in recent years, my vision has drastically changed. I have gone from being able to use the smallest of print in Bibles to not being able to clearly read giant print. Thank God for glasses that enable me to still read.

If you ever question the importance of vision, just close your eyes and try to walk around your house. You will very quickly understand the importance of eyesight. Those who cannot see at all live in a world that is far different than the seeing people live in. Their world is one of darkness and vulnerability to falling, to being hit by a car, or many other harmful things.

Yes, vision is very important, but there is another kind of vision that is equally or more important. In Proverbs 29:18 (KJV), the Bible says, "Where there is no vision, the people perish." The kind of vision spoken of in this verse is a mental picture of something that you want to happen in your life. It is this kind of vision that translates into passion, and passion is the driving force behind every great thing that is done. Great artists have a vision in their mind of what they want their completed artwork to look like, and they have a passion to make it happen. It is the vision of a cure for a terrible disease that gives the researcher a passion to work long hours and perhaps to give his life to the pursuit of that dream. Without vision, the Bible says people perish. How do they perish? They perish because of an absence of hope. Without vision, all they can hope for is more of the same, and life becomes a dull routine.

In the physical realm, vision occurs when the baby is born. Many times, the same is true in the spiritual world. When someone is born again, God places the seed of vision in the new convert's heart. When Saul (later Paul) was on his way to Damascus to persecute Christians, Jesus spoke to him and struck him blind. God gave him a vision of a man named Ananias coming to help him and then began to reveal the genesis of His plan for the great apostle (see Acts 9:1-19).

To use another analogy, the unbeliever lives in darkness. When he is born into the kingdom, enough light is turned on in the room so that he can see a basic outline of things that he has never seen before. It is over a period of time spent walking with God that his vision becomes more and more clear. Those things that in the early days he thought he should do, now he knows for certain he should do.

Proverbs 4:18 says, "The path of the righteous is like the first gleam of dawn, shining ever brighter till the full light of day." Later in his life, Paul knew exactly what his God-given mission was, as seen in Romans 1:1, "Paul, a servant of Christ Jesus, called to be an apostle and set apart for the gospel of God." There is no ambiguity in that statement. He knew that he was a servant of Christ Jesus, that he was an apostle who had been set apart for the gospel of God.

The importance of a clear spiritual vision cannot be underestimated. After all, everyone is headed in some direction. People who know God's plan for their lives move ahead purposely. It is these people who are more likely to come to the end of their lives with a sense of satisfaction that life has had meaning because they have done what they were born to do. On the other hand, those who drift through life without a clear vision are more likely to come to the end of their lives wondering what should have been or could have been. They have drifted through life, and now there is no way to go back and do it over again. Vision, on the other hand, is like a compass that keeps you moving in the direction of God's plan. It allows you to see that desired thing before comes to pass. If you can't see it in the present, it is likely that you will never experience it in the future.

How then does one obtain this vision that is so vital in having a life full of God's blessings? First, there must be a willing heart. When Saul was converted on the Damascus Road, he was ready to lay his life down for the One he had formerly persecuted. He totally gave his life to the call of God. In Acts 9:20, the Scriptures say, "At once he began to preach in the synagogues that Jesus is the Son of God." God reveals His vision to the kind of person who has that kind of open heart.

Let me encourage you to receive God's vision for your life and to do it now. By faith, take one step at a time and walk toward the light of God's unique call on your life.

Lord, today we ask You to give us open hearts that are willing to receive Your vision for our lives. Help us to understand that You will give us the power and the ability to do what You have for us to accomplish. We are weak, but You are strong. Help us, we pray in Jesus's name. Amen.

CHAPTER 39

THE BATTLE STILL RAGES

I f you are a nature lover, you would probably enjoy visiting Chattanooga, Tennessee. While in Chattanooga, you can take a drive up Lookout Mountain and observe the beautiful foliage and a magnificent view. On your left, you see the winding Tennessee River, and to your right, you see beautiful huge trees, grass, and vegetation of all kinds. If you happen to visit during the fall, you will see the leaves as they turn different shades of colors from light yellow to dark red and even bronze.

Chattanooga also has a number of tourist attractions that are worth seeing. One of the more awesome places to visit is the Chickamauga and Chattanooga National Military Park. The Battle of Chickamauga has been called the bloodiest two days in American history. Casualties numbered around 34,000 with thousands dead. There is something solemn about walking around many hundreds of graves where those faithful men gave their lives. You can almost picture in your mind's eye the ferocious fighting that happened between the North and the South on the ground where you are standing. You can almost feel the ground shaking under your feet as thousands of men ran to meet the enemy in deadly combat. It is as though the wind still echoes the cries of men as they sought to stay alive while under brutal attack. With your imagination, you can hear the booming of the cannon along with the sound of many rifles.

Close your eyes and envision the ground being littered with the bodies of soldiers who were alive fifteen minutes before but who have now entered eternity to spend either with God or without Him. It is the battlefield where victories are won or lost. It is on the battlefield that the futures of men and their families are sealed.

The greatest battlefield, however, resides not on the mountain or in the valley. The greatest battlefield exists in the minds of people like you and me, and unlike the battle at Chickamauga, the fighting never ceases. It rages within your heart from morning until night. This is a spiritual battle. It is not between human beings. It is between human beings and spiritual beings. Satan and his demonic army are ever on the watch for someone whom they can attack with their evil schemes: "Be self-controlled and alert. Your enemy the devil prowls around like a roaring lion looking for someone to devour" (1 Peter 5:8). The devil's objective is to capture your mind because he knows that if you think wrong, you will do wrong.

As we face this never-ceasing battle, we must understand that in every case, the thought is the father of the deed. In other words, someone does not do wrong until he has first thought wrong. Genesis 6:5 (KJV) records the lifestyle of ancient people on earth: "And God saw that the wickedness of man was great in the earth, and that every imagination of the thoughts of his heart was only evil continually." Their wickedness was great because their thoughts were evil. Later on, the man Samson was specially chosen by God to deliver his people from the Philistines, but Samson thought wrong, and as a result, he did wrong. The same is true of David, Solomon, and many others.

Many good men and women have been defeated by the adversary because they allowed their minds to think in unbiblical ways. As

Proverbs 23:7 says, "For as he thinks in his heart, so he is." According to that well-known Scripture, what you are today is the result of yesterday's thinking, and what you will be tomorrow is being determined by your thoughts today.

The Battle of Chickamauga was a horrible event, but no more horrible than the spiritual battle that we face. If we could pull back the curtain and look into the spiritual world and observe the spiritual battle that is ever present, we would see something more terrible than we could possibly imagine.

To think of hideous spiritual beings filled with rage and anger toward God's people is truly a frightening thing. Ephesians 6:12 plainly states, "For our struggle is not against flesh and blood, but against the rulers, against the authorities, against the powers of this dark world and against the spiritual forces of evil in the heavenly realms." It is because of these unseen "spiritual forces of evil" that verse 13 says, "Therefore put on the whole armor of God, so that when the day of evils comes, you may be able to stand your ground, and after you have done everything, to stand." Without the armor of God, we are easy prey for the wicked one.

When the devil attacks your mind, you must answer with faith. Faith looks at negative circumstances and believes in God's ability and faithfulness to do what seems to be the undoable. So the battle rages. The spiritual cannons are booming, and spiritual rifles are aimed at your mind. If you open your mind to those spiritual bullets, you will be a spiritual casualty.

The truth is that life for you will become what you allow your mind to think on. The message of 2 Corinthians 10:4-5 is vital if we are to be victorious in the battle:

The weapons we fight with are not the weapons of the world. On the contrary, they have divine power to demolish strongholds. We demolish arguments and every pretension that sets itself up against the knowledge of God, and we take captive every thought to make it obedient to Christ.

If you will take every thought captive for Christ, you will never be taken captive by the evil one. Remember, the battlefield is in your mind, so fight your spiritual battle with spiritual weapons. Your life depends on it.

Dear God, please help us to draw near to You so that You may protect us from the spiritual forces of wickedness that we cannot see, that we may stand firm. Amen.

CHAPTER 40

ALL THINGS?

S ome things are really hard to believe. For example, the well-known verse Romans 8:28 clearly says, "And we know that in all things God works for the good of those who love him, who have been called according to his purpose." If I get a raise at work or get a new job with higher pay, then Romans 8:28 is easy to believe. I needed the extra money, and God, who loves me and can do all things, provided for me. That is easy enough to understand.

On that basis, maybe we ought to all adopt Romans 8:28 as our favorite verse. Isn't it a great thing that God makes all good things work together for our benefit? There is, however, a big problem because that verse does not say all *positive* things work together for our good. To the contrary, it is talking about all things—both good and bad. It is just as much for the suffering believer who does not know where his next paycheck will come from as it is for those who may be enjoying sufficient funds. And the believer who is sick and in the hospital has just as much claim on Romans 8:28 as does the person who is in perfect health. That leaves us in a dilemma because we know what good and bad is—at least we think we do—and what is going on in our lives at the present time may seem to be anything but good. How is it a good thing to endure a prolonged illness that leaves you trapped in a body that will not function properly? How is it good to pray to the Father about a certain issue and not receive an answer to your prayer?

Most of us could tell our own stories about how God allowed us to go through some very deep waters in order that He may do something good for us when we finally come out of those depths. I experienced such a situation shortly after I graduated from Bible college. The door was opened for me to work in an established church as an associate pastor, so my pregnant wife, our little girl, and I loaded up a U-Haul trailer and traveled to a city and state that we had never even visited. The church people were excited for us to be there, and we enjoyed the sights and activities that this particular part of the country had to offer.

In some ways, it was a memorable experience, but the longer I stayed there, the more I began seeing that the pastor and I had some fundamental differences concerning the church's philosophy of ministry. The last thing I wanted to do was to cause any problems, so I decided the best thing for me to do was to leave.

My grandmother's house was not being occupied, so my little family went back to east Texas to stay in her house until I was called by a church to be its pastor. I had no idea what was waiting for me. I waited for fourteen months before I had the opportunity to go back into full-time ministry. Each day was excruciatingly painful, and things seemed impossible. I guess if I learned anything through that very difficult time, it is the fact that when you think you are at your breaking point and can't go any further, you can. When everything within you is screaming, "I can't take anymore," you can. I know what it is to go through the dark night of the soul. I know what it is to be surrounded by people and yet to feel very lonely. I know the feeling of thinking that everyone else in life is passing me by while I sit beside Job and scratch my wounds. I was so down that I would have had to look way up to see the bottom.

Mentally I still believed that God was in control, but to be quite honest, it did not seem like He was anywhere to be found. Where was God? God was where He always has been. He was sitting on the throne providentially doing what was best for His children. Where was God? God was in the spiritual gym with one of His sons giving him a workout so that he could become stronger and more useful in ministry. First Peter 5:10 says, "And the God of all grace, who called you to his eternal glory in Christ, after you have suffered a little while, will himself restore you and make you strong, firm and steadfast." Many times in life, we learn more retrospectively than we do when we are going through difficult times. God is more than able to win the battle, but sometimes He needs to prepare His soldiers so they will be capable of fighting for Him. I learned many things through that horrible time. I learned that God is listening when it seems as though He is not. Just as a mother would hear the slightest cry of her baby, God hears the cries of His people. It is not always chastisement that keeps us in the unwanted predicament that we long to be freed from. Rather it is the mercy of God that keeps us there. That is because God is taking that almost unbearable circumstance and molding our lives so that we become less like ourselves and more like Jesus.

God's conflicts are won by faith, and faith grows through trusting when you cannot see and obeying when you do not want to. It grows when you would rather do anything other than what you are doing, and when you desperately want the burden removed from your shoulders. We think that if God would just allow us to see how things are going to turn out in the end, then maybe we could endure the hardships that threaten to sink us. Our thinking is that we could bear the burden if we only knew how it is going to work for our good.

God does not reveal those things, because Hebrews 11:1 (KJV) tells us that "faith is the substance of things hoped for, the evidence of things not seen." Knowing what God has in store might give us comfort in the immediate, but we would lose the spiritual growth that we would gain if we finish the rocky, thorn-infested course God has us on. And when God does finally show Himself real, He usually delivers us in such a way that there is no doubt in our mind that God has answered. The fruit of the trial is that we become stronger and more able to be a spiritual warrior than we would ever would have been if we not been through the fire.

So Romans 8:28 is true. All things do work together for the good of God's people. One day, we will be in heaven, and when we look back upon our earthly existence, we will understand that the things which at the time seemed to be the most difficult—the things that brought us to the point of despair—these were really the things that made us who we became for God. Praise God for His infinite wisdom, His unlimited patience, and His unrelenting pursuit of a deeper relationship with His much loved people.

Dear God, we need Your help so desperately because we do not understand. So many times, the things that bring us the greatest joy are preceded by things that bring us the most heartaches. Strengthen us that we would believe that You know what is best and that You are indeed making all things work together for the good in our lives. Thank You in Jesus's name. Amen.

CHAPTER 41

THE WOODEN CAR

S ome children's books begin with a line like: "Long, long ago, there was an old woman who lived in a forest." I am going to change that line. My line reads like this: "Long, long ago, there was a young boy who lived in a neighborhood." And then comes the rest of the story . . .

The young boy decided one day that he would build a wooden car. The first step was to gather up the materials that he needed, so he got some wood, wheels, nails, and even some rope, and then went to work. He just knew that it was going to be a fine car that he would have a lot of fun with. He built the frame and then a steering device that consisted of a board that was movable and that could be directed by the pull of a rope on either side, but he needed more. He had to have a brake for the car, so he nailed another board in a position that would enable him to apply pressure on the car's back wheel.

According to the plan, if the board had enough pressure applied to it, he could slow the car down and even stop it if necessary. The young man worked and worked on the car until it was finished, and what a fine car it was! He just knew that he would have a great time with one of the finest crafted and engineered vehicles ever made. Right next to his house, there was a road that consisted of a steep slope, and the young boy's plan was to drive his new invention down that hill.

The long-awaited day came. He expected it to be a day of glory as he successfully completed his ride down the hill. No doubt, news would spread of his great accomplishment, and soon the whole neighborhood would be gathered to watch the exhibition of his second ride down the steep slope. The time came, and he was ready. One thing yet remained to be done. He needed a witness. He needed someone who would see his victorious and glorious ride, and who would be able to tell others of his skill, courage, and vision. So he chose his younger brother to be his witness. The plan was simple. While he was driving his car, his younger brother would ride along beside him on his bicycle.

The car was positioned, and the brave young inventor settled down into the wonderful car he had built. Knowing that he was about to witness a historical event, the younger brother intensely awaited the start of this exciting adventure that was sure to be talked about for generations to come. The brilliant young inventor was determined to succeed, and with the taste of victory already in his mouth, he shoved off in the car—and it all began.

It didn't take long for the soon-to-be-famous car to begin gathering speed. As the little brother rode alongside his older and wiser brother, he, too, felt the thrill of adrenaline rushing through his body. Faster and faster the wooden car traveled. In fact, it began moving a little too fast, but that was okay because the brake had been installed and was ready for use. The young engineer applied the brake, and as he did, the car began slowing down. There was, however, a problem. It was soon apparent that the wooden brake was not sufficient to keep up with the increased speed of his wooden vehicle. The young genius pushed harder and harder on the brake as the car continued to move faster and faster and faster. He pushed the brake with all of his might, and then the unthinkable happened. The wooden brake broke. That's right. There was no way possible to slow down the ever-increasing speed of the potential casket that he was riding in. His little brother pumped harder and harder to keep up with the car as it raced down the hill, and then the unthinkable happened again. The wooden car, which had been so carefully constructed, hit the curb at the bottom of the hill and literally exploded into pieces and left the young boy lying on the ground. Though by the grace of God he lived to see another day, he learned some valuable lessons as to what not to do.

That wooden car which promised so much had some deadly flaws. The young man was deceived into thinking he could slow it down anytime he wanted and that all would be well. He had no idea that the car would become uncontrollable, and he certainly was not thinking about the consequences of what would happen if he hit the curb at the bottom of the hill.

Now that I have grown up and have lived life for a while, I can see some parallels between the car I made and the sin in our lives. Just as the wooden car had its beginning in my mind, so it is with sin. Sin originates in our thinking and then begins to take form in our actions. As I built that wooden car, I thought I had everything under control. I installed a brake that would slow me down if need be, but neither my car nor sin is able to be slowed down once it begins moving. Sin moves faster and faster in one's life until it is totally out of control and headed for a crash at the bottom. The only way to avoid the crash with sin is to stay away from it. Sin looks fun, and the Scriptures say that it is pleasurable for a season (see Hebrews 11:25). The season of enjoyment, however, is soon over, and the inevitable crash occurs.

I was fortunate that I was not injured seriously. Many who enter the car of sin are not so fortunate. For them, the ride ends in disaster. The best thing is to listen closely to the instructions God gives us and to build according to His plans. We are only safe when we are riding in the car He designs.

Lord, You have spared us from being destroyed by our sin many times. Today we ask for Your wisdom to guide us in our future. Help us to stay out of the car of sin and to ride in the car of your safety. We need you. Amen.

CHAPTER 42

CHANGING CHURCH, UNCHANGING GOD

Anyone who knows church history understands the fact that the church throughout the ages has had its ups and downs. There have been times when the church was so steeped in ritualism and religiosity that it would seem as though it was nearly dead. And then, by the grace of God, revival fires began to burn, and the church returned, at least to some extent, to its roots and intended purpose.

It is like the "sin cycle" found in the book of Judges. When the people ignored the true God and worshipped idols, God sent judgment. After some time, the people would cry out to God for deliverance, and He would send them a deliverer who would free them from the bondage they had incurred by their unbelief and sin. They rejoiced in the victory God gave, but inevitably they began to slide back down into the mud of sin, and the cycle began all over again.

Many years ago, I heard a Christian leader make the statement that his era was a very strange time for Christians. That dear man would not believe what is happening today. Christianity on the current scene in America is a very ambiguous practice. On the one hand, you have the legalists who are ready to renounce anyone who does not live according to their self-devised standards. Such man-made rules are a real turnoff to the non-Christian, but legalism is probably not the greatest problem we face. The greatest problem we face is probably just the opposite. Somehow Christians seem to have forgotten that we serve a God who is holy and that he asks us to reflect him by also being holy (see 1 Peter 1:15-16).

It is astounding to see the current Christian generation accepting things that are plainly condemned in Scripture. It is not at all uncommon for some Christian groups to go to a Bible study and then after the study to go to a bar. Sexual immorality is accepted as normal among many of those who claim Christ. What's more, we are raising a generation of pastors who do not understand biblical theology and some who openly deny the truth of the Word. The result is multitudes being led away.

The time has come for those who love the Lord to stand for what the Lord loves and to reject what He hates. The time has come for Bible-believing Christians to come out of the "closet" and announce their allegiance to the purity demanded by Almighty God. Believers must recognize that living a godly life is a privilege, not a burden.

The "numbers game" has led many pastors to believe that big is better regardless of what is lived. God is not glorified because we have more breathing bodies in the auditorium. God is only glorified when His people reflect His nature. God desires people who will be the bright lights that expose sin. He wants people who are firmly rooted in His Word and who model godliness. Our standards are not to be set by the actions of the majority, for the majority is usually wrong. God is not impressed when the church becomes "cool" in order to reach a decadent society. God commends the church that follows His commission to make disciples of Jesus Christ, not just attenders but disciples. Anything less than the fulfillment of that commission is failure to be obedient. When all has been done on earth, we must give an account for how we have lived. It will be obvious at that point as to whether we have sought to please man or to please God.

Lord, You are our only hope. Protect us from compromise and help us to live a holy life. In Jesus's name. Amen.

CHAPTER 43

MISUNDERSTANDING

"I can't believe that you said that to me!"

"What are you talking about? I didn't say that!"

"Yes you did!"

"You have totally misunderstood what I said!"

"I heard exactly what you said!"

"That is not what I meant!"

"Then why did you say it?"

This fictitious conversation is a classic example of misunderstanding. The offended person feels that he has been verbally attacked, and the offender feels frustrated, angry, and mistreated. In reality, it does not matter what you say to someone. What matters is what they think that you said. The old saying, "Perception is reality," can be damaging. People have lost their jobs, their marriages, and their peace of mind because of a misunderstanding.

Once as a young boy, my mother asked me to help her do something, and I was not excited about her idea to enlist me in her project. My mother said something like, "You need to help." I was wrong, but I murmured something like, "Oh, help." I must not have pronounced the "p" on the end of the word "help" very well, because my mother thought that I had said another word, and she went ballistic. Whirling around, she said, "What did you say?" She was ready to beat me with a whip or have me locked up in some institution. We did not talk that way in our home, and she was not about to let it get started. I knew that I had not used that bad word, but it sounded to her like I did. That's the kind of stuff misunderstandings are made of. Make no mistake about it, misunderstandings do happen, and they happen regularly.

Even Jesus was misunderstood on numerous occasions. One notable incident was at the time of Lazarus's death. John 11:1-6 says:

> Now a man named Lazarus was sick. He was from Bethany, the village of Mary and her sister Martha. This Mary, whose brother Lazarus now lay sick, was the same one who poured perfume on the Lord and wiped his feet with her hair. So the sisters sent word to Jesus, "Lord, the one you love is sick." When he heard this, Jesus said, "This sickness will not end in death. No, it is for God's glory so that God's Son may be glorified through it." Jesus loved Martha and her sister and Lazarus. Yet when he heard that Lazarus was sick, he stayed where he was two more days.

How would you have understood the response of Jesus? Your brother is sick and about to die, and you know that if Jesus would come, He could heal him. But that is not what happened. When Jesus heard that Lazarus was sick, He stayed where He was for two days. That would have been a confusing situation to say the least. I am sure that even the Lord's disciples questioned what he was doing. It did not seem right, and it was not in keeping with what they knew of their Master. The situation would appear to be like a man who is sitting on a couch watching a football game, and he receives a call from the hospital informing him that his wife was in an accident and has been hospitalized in critical condition. Instead of jumping up off of the couch, grabbing his keys, and driving frantically to the hospital, the

141

man goes to the refrigerator, gets a piece of pie and a glass of milk, and then finishes watching the football game. That is about the way Jesus's apparent lack of concern would have seemed. The Lord's delay in coming to heal their brother must have left the two sisters Mary and Martha hurt and perplexed.

Why would He wait in a life-or-death situation? A similar situation took place with the disciples as they sought to cross the Sea of Galilee and were almost killed in a terrible storm, which we looked at in an earlier chapter. As we saw, Mark 4:38 says, "Jesus was in the stern, sleeping on a cushion. The disciples woke Him and said to Him, 'Teacher, don't you care if we drown?'" In both the case of Lazarus and the case of the disciples, God seemed to be uncaring and unconcerned, but He was not. The reality of the matter was that, in both cases, God was about to do an awesome, never-to-be-forgotten miracle that is still being talked about to this day.

Isn't it strange that we are so quick to lose our faith regardless of the fact that God has never failed us. The same kind of thing has no doubt played out in our lives thousands of times. We have been in a terrible trial, but when we call out to Jesus for help, He seemingly does nothing. In our pain, we cry out with the disciples, "Don't you care?" Yes, Jesus does care, but He often wraps his best gifts in a cloak of misunderstanding. If Jesus had gone immediately and healed Lazarus, some might have even claimed that he wasn't really dead. But when someone has been in the grave for four days, and he walks out perfectly well, you know that God has shown up in an undeniable manner.

So often, like Mary, Martha, and the disciples, we misunderstand what God is doing in our lives. The truth is that we should expect to misunderstand. Didn't God say in Isaiah 55:8, "For my thoughts are not your thoughts, neither are your ways my ways"? While the two sisters were misunderstanding Jesus's intentions, He was more concerned than we will ever be able to understand, and He is just as concerned about you. It is when we wait in faith that we are able to witness the glory of God as He does the undoable in answer to our prayers.

Lord God, we know that we do not see things the way You do. Your vision is perfect, but ours is blurred. Help us so that when we cannot see, we will trust in You as You are and always have been. In Jesus's name. Amen.

CHAPTER 44

AMERICA'S REAL PROBLEM

Have you ever put together a giant puzzle? When you begin the process, nothing even remotely resembles a picture. Then there is that almost magical piece of the puzzle that when connected to another piece causes you to begin seeing something. At first, it may be only vaguely familiar, but as you continue to work, you suddenly see something that is recognizable.

Memories of growing up are much like putting together a puzzle. Sometimes certain thoughts in your mind connect, and you begin remembering something that you have not thought of for many years. If enough pieces come together in your mind, you are almost able to see that particular part of your life that is long gone. Looking closely, I put in another piece, and it is beginning to make sense. That is me behind our redwood fence down at the creek catching tadpoles. After some more work, I see myself picking blackberries, and soon my mother is making a blackberry cobbler. The more complete the puzzle becomes, the more I see something more than just individual events in my life. I begin to remember the environment that I had the privilege of growing up in. It was a good time, a peaceful time. It was a time when hard-working people built a great society. Then I begin to realize that I don't live in that world anymore. America, as I knew it as a boy, was much different than it is today. To my generation, it was a normal thing to have prayer at school. My high school even had Bible class taught by the principal's wife. Although I know that there were people who did not believe in God or the Bible, I personally never met anyone who didn't. Today many people live in fear of terrorist attacks. I never knew of anything like that.

As I sit writing this devotional, it is an election year, and both candidates are eagerly pursuing the goal of the presidency. It is the usual political rhetoric that you hear on television, in which one side is bashing the other side and both claim to have the answer to America's difficulties. The real problem of America today, however, is not the political battle between Democrats and Republicans. Our true problems are moral and spiritual. Many if not most people have adopted the view of secularism that tells us man is at the center of the universe, not God. We are living in the midst of many thousands of people who believe that there is no such thing as absolute truth. Everything is relative, and truth is what you think it to be.

There is a certain sadness in my heart as I continue to put pieces together and see the images from years ago. I see how it used to be in this great nation and how it is now as we live in a decaying society. The upside of all of that is that God knows what to do about decay and spiritual and moral darkness. In Mathew 5:13-16, Jesus said,

> "You are the salt of the earth. But if the salt loses its saltiness, how can it be made salty again? It is no longer good for anything, except to be thrown out and trampled by men. You are the light of the world. A city on a hill cannot be hidden. Neither do people light a lamp and put it under a bowl. Instead they put it on its stand, and it gives light to everyone in the house. In the same way, let your light shine before men, that they may see your good deeds and praise your Father in heaven."

In those words spoken over 2,000 years ago by Jesus, we have the answer to all that ails us. If we are the salt of the earth, we will preserve the society from decay. If we become the light of the world, we will shine God's truth into a biblically illiterate nation. People will once again know truth, and we will elect officials who possess honor and integrity.

Our biggest problem is not those who do not believe in God. Our biggest problem is those who do believe. We who believe the truth of the Word of God have not lived what we believe. Instead of being used by the Holy Spirit to change our world, all too often we have allowed the world to change us. It seems as though the younger generation of Christians want to be "cool," when in reality, we should be holy.

Leviticus 18:1-4 (NLT) makes it plain:

> Then the LORD said to Moses, "Give the following instructions to the people of Israel. I am the LORD your God. So do not act like the people in Egypt, where you used to live, or like the people of Canaan, where I am taking you. You must not imitate their way of life. You must obey all my regulations and be careful to obey my decrees, for I am the LORD your God."

When we conform to the culture, instead of changing it, we lose our seasoning. I believe that if the Christians in America would truly have revival in their hearts so that they served God wholeheartedly, God in His mercy would remove His hand of judgment and allow us to once again experience His favor. The puzzle of life as it now stands in America does not have to continue in the same direction. God can turn it around so that right once again becomes right, and wrong once again becomes wrong. Through the mercy and grace of God, we can once again become a nation who can truly say, "In God we trust." If you are willing to become a part of the solution, start today by allowing

God to control your life so that you may truly be salt and light. That, my friend, is the only hope that we have.

Almighty God, we confess today our willful sin against You and ask for Your forgiveness. We ask that You will have mercy upon us and our nation and turn the hearts of people back to You. We do not deserve what we ask for, but we believe in Your mercy. Help us, we pray in Jesus's name. Amen.

CHAPTER 45

DIRTY HANDS

Most people know what it means to have dirty hands. Those who create artwork from clay know the experience of immersing their hands in the clay until their hands are more mud than they are hands. Maybe you have worked in a flower bed digging in dirt so that you can plant something that you hope to one day be beautiful. Whatever the case, sometimes we have to be willing to get our hands dirty before we can create something of worth and beauty.

What is true of working with clay or in the soil is also true of society. People today are longing for something better. They long for a civilization where the fear of being robbed, cheated, or physically harmed is not an issue. People are hungry and thirsty to be able to not live in fear of their children being taken advantage of by some unscrupulous person, but in most cases, we don't seem to be making any progress.

I am old enough to remember a time when we never locked the doors to our homes or cars. We left the windows open at night and left the job of cooling the house to a rumbling attic fan. The neighborhood that I lived in had a network of friends, and in the afternoons, the mothers would sit on their front yards in lawn chairs in the midst of soft green grass, tall pine trees, and singing birds. While mothers chatted about their lives, problems, and triumphs, and the latest news, their children would ride their bicycles up and down the street. Everyone was having a great time, and everyone felt safe.

As the years have flown by, our society has undergone a metamorphosis. Gone are the days when one does not lock his car or his house. In fact, we do more than lock doors. We now have alarm systems on our homes, so that we may be awakened if visited by an intruder. The feeling of safety has been replaced with gangs, drugs, and drive-by shootings. Many live in gated communities, and some have metal bars across their windows. Many people long for the days of relative peace and safety, and wish that we could openly coexist with other human beings, but where would we begin to look for such a haven of rest?

Most good things don't come easy. Most good things require getting our hands dirty. That is true in our world, and it is especially true in the church. God intends His church to be a place of refuge for His people. It is there, in the community of those who have been washed and made clean by the blood of Jesus, that people should find the peace and safety they so want to have. It is in that body of believers that those who are older in the faith should reach out with open arms to receive those who have just escaped from the filthiness and defilement of sin. Ephesians 5:26 tells us that the Word of God is a cleansing agent that can make pure the dirtiness of sinners. It says we are sanctified and cleansed "by the washing with water through the word." God's plan is that those who have been changed by the truth of His Word should pass on that cleansing truth to others who are not as mature in their faith.

I remember experiencing such affirmation and love from the first church I attended after having become a Christian. The good people of that church received me with open arms and made me feel like I had been a part of their family forever. I soon developed relationships with people who truly felt like family, people whom I knew I could count on to be there for me regardless of the need I was facing at the moment. I wasn't perfectly clean by a long shot, but that was okay. Those people loved me anyway, and their love motivated me to continue to be cleaner.

In 1 John 3:18, the apostle John said, "Dear children, let us not love with words or tongue but with actions and in truth." John was saying, "Don't just talk about love. Show it by getting involved in the lives of others!" Reaching out to people is far from being a sanitary procedure, and it requires a willingness on your part to get your hands dirty. It would be much easier to sit back in a sterile environment wearing a spotless white robe and admiring the clean, shiny halo over your head, but that is not our Lord's way. He was so willing to get His hands dirty that He has been called the "friend of sinners."

Unlike the pious Pharisees who thought themselves too good to reach down and touch the lives of dirty people, Jesus got in the mud pit so that He could lift others out. If you follow His example, you can expect to at times to become emotionally, physically, and spiritually drained as you seek to help others to clean up their lives, but we cannot forsake our calling. God's plan is not to place us behind glass in a museum of saints. We have been called to fight in the trenches for the sake of His glorious name. Are you willing to get your hands dirty?

Lord, we ask You to help us make a difference for You in this world. Help us to be willing to get our hands dirty. In Jesus's name, we pray.

CHAPTER 46

FAILURE

O f all of those experiences that we have in life, failure is one of the hardest to deal with. In fact, we would probably rather not even have that word in our vocabulary. Failure hurts. It demoralizes us and whispers in our ear that we are not as good as those who have succeeded. Failure makes us feel inferior and takes the joy out of living.

The real truth is that everyone fails at one point or another. Even the great biblical heroes that we hold in such high esteem had their share of failure. Moses, the great lawgiver, had his failures, such as when he hit the rock with his staff instead of speaking to it as God had told him to do (see Numbers 20:1-12).

Elijah was a fearless prophet of God who challenged a whole nation to a contest on Mount Carmel, as we saw in an earlier chapter. He could have easily been killed by a pagan nation that wanted him out of the way, but there was no hesitancy on his part to stand alone for the God he trusted in. The story of his victory on Mount Carmel is legendary (see 1 Kings 18:16-40). After the prophets of Baal had cried out to their god and even inflicted bodily harm on themselves in order to get his attention, this man Elijah stepped up to the plate and called upon the real God, who then answered with a blast of fire that consumed the sacrifice. Elijah knew how to succeed, but he also knew how to fail. After the showdown between the false prophets and Jehovah, we see our man Elijah running into the desert in fear of Queen Jezebel (see 1 Kings 19:1-5). He was depressed, lonely, and defeated.

David, the man after God's own heart, was the most successful king that Israel ever had. He was a mighty man in battle. He was a man who trusted God to deliver him in impossible situations, such as his battle with Goliath. You can add to those things the fact that he was a skilled musician and the writer of many psalms that have been used through the years to turn the hearts of people to worship God. Yes, David was a great man who knew what it was to succeed, but he also knew what it was to fail, like the time he committed adultery and murder (see 2 Samuel 11). When we fail, we often feel as though we are the only ones who ever experienced it, but that is far from being the truth. The truth is that everyone fails at some time and that failure is just as much a part of life as is success.

James 3:2 says, "We all stumble in many ways." Nothing could be any more true. In fact, some of us seem to do more stumbling than we do walking, but that's okay. As much as it would seem otherwise, failure can be one of our greatest friends. It is able to get our attention and turn our hearts to God, and it does a very good job of teaching us humility.

Isaiah 38:12-15 says:

"Like a shepherd's tent my house
    has been pulled down and taken from me.
Like a weaver I have rolled up my life,
    and he has cut me off from the loom;
        day and night you made an end of me.
I waited patiently till dawn,
    but like a lion he broke all my bones;

day and night you made an end of me.
I cried like a swift or thrush,
I moaned like a mourning dove.
My eyes grew weak as I looked to the heavens.
I am troubled; O Lord, come to my aid!
But what can I say?
He has spoken to me, and he himself has done this.
I will walk humbly all my years
because of this anguish of my soul."

Sometimes God allows us to fail so badly that the memory of that failure remains with us for the rest of our lives. It becomes a safeguard against pride. When pride raises its ugly head, God reminds us of our great failure and turns our thinking back to him. As long as I think that I can do it without God, I probably will try. Failure urges me to not try to do by myself what has already caused me great pain. The pain of the failure outweighs the satisfaction of trying to do it myself. I realize that without God, I can do nothing.

Great failures produce great humility. Remember that God does not waste our pain. He uses it to teach us things that we would never learn otherwise. After He teaches me that I can't, He teaches me that He can. Do you remember the story of the disciples who had fished all night long and caught nothing (see Luke 5:1-7)? Jesus, standing on the shore, told them to let their nets down again. That is something that they probably would not have done for any other person, but since it was Jesus telling them to do it, they obeyed, and you know what happened: they caught so many fish that they almost sunk the boat.

Failure, then, teaches us one of the greatest lessons of life: we can't, but He can. That one lesson is a foundation upon which many lessons can be built. We can't, but He can. In a world that is overcome with darkness, can you really find a mate who will want to live a godly life with you? Can you really raise godly children in an X-rated society?

Can you maintain your integrity on the job when no one else seems to care? Can you climb out of the financial hole you find yourself trapped in? The answer is the same: we can't, but He can.

Lord God, help us to never forget the lesson that failure brings with it, and help us to never underestimate Your great ability to do whatever needs to be done. We pray in Jesus's name. Amen.

CHAPTER 47

LIVING IN THE NOW

Of all of the things that we experience in life, aging is one of the most perplexing. When you don't have it, you want it. But when you get it, you don't want it.

Those who don't have age look forward to getting it because they feel that it will bring respect, freedom, and importance. To no longer be thought of as a child, to be able to go where you want to go when you want to go, is surely one of the greatest things imaginable. To lose the bondage of parental restraint and to know the freedom of adulthood is certainly an enviable state of living. If one were an adult, he could eat whatever he wanted. Ice cream could become a vegetable, and soft drinks could become fresh-squeezed juice. Without question, this is the way to live! If only time would move faster, or if we could wake up tomorrow morning and suddenly be ten years older, how great that would be!

On the other hand, those who have paid their dues through the passing of years now long for bygone days. If for only one day, one could go back to being a child with boundless energy. To once again have the privilege of dreaming of a preferred future and looking forward to what we something we desperately want to happen. To think about playing Little League baseball, to once again be a cheerleader, or to play in the school band would be a dream come true. Knowing the security of being provided for and taken care of by parents who love you would remove the stress that so often steals our joy, and would return a feeling of safety and security that we have not known for many, many years. Having the privilege of a roof over our head, food on the table, and nice clothes to wear without having to work for them would be such a glorious gift. To once again enjoy sleepovers and dream about the future would surely be wonderful.

Thoughts like that may be fun to entertain in the fantasies of our minds, but they obviously will do no good. To each of us, there is dealt a deck of cards that spell out our destinies, and those destinies are divided up into seasons of time. You cannot choose which season of life you are in. You can only embrace it as a positive thing, or try to run from it, but in the final analysis, you are unable to change anything. To wish for an age when you are young or to wish for youth when you are old is an exercise in futility that can only guarantee one thing: you will never be happy.

Trying to escape one of life's seasons is like trying to skip the beauty of spring, the fun times of summer, the beauty of autumn leaves, or the challenge of winter activities. If it is youthful springtime in your life, rest in the security of parents who love you, because there will come a time when they will have no seasons left and their journey will be finished. Take advantage of your spring because, although it will never be forgotten, it will also never be repeated. Enjoy the new growth on trees, flowers, and other plants because it will soon be gone. If you are in the summer of your life, enjoy the activities that are available to you, and be diligent in preparing for future seasons. If you are in the fall of life, your children are probably grown, and you have more time to pursue things that you could not be involved in when you were taking care of your little ones. If you are in the winter of your life, thank God for the wisdom that He has given you, and pass on that which you have learned to the next generation.

It is an unfortunate thing that we often do not understand the value of the various seasons of life until we have passed them by. We need to remember that this life is not a "dress rehearsal." It is the real thing, and it is moving on with each successive day. As we step into each new day, we have the opportunity to make the most of the hours we are given. Those hours can be used to bless our lives, to help other people, and to honor God through a Christ-like life. Such opportunities offer themselves to the willing, but they will not plead for your involvement and are reluctant to offer second chances.

Don't miss the seasons of your life. They have been given by God to each of us, and we can either use them or lose them. The choice is ours. There is, however, one encouraging thought beyond the seasons of life. If you know Jesus Christ personally, when your final season of this life is over, life for you will only be starting. You will find yourself transitioning into a new kind of season, a season not composed of seconds, minutes, hours, days, or even years. The season of life beyond this earthly realm is an eternal one that will never pass away. You may have come into the kingdom in a late season of your life so that you missed much you could have had. If so, be encouraged, for you will not miss the glory of the eternal season. It is a season of your existence when all that is bad will be banished and when good will forever prevail. Our God is gracious! Spend time praising Him for that which is to come, and live out the rest of your days on earth to their fullest. The time draws near!

God, we ask you to help us to live each season of our lives fully. Help us to not long for some other time, but to take advantage of the "now" that we are a part of. Give us strength to give You glory with each passing day. For Christ's sake, we pray. Amen.

CHAPTER 48

PRAYER

O f all the things that are common to man, prayer stands at the forefront. Somehow even in spite of the fall of man, there remains a yearning to be in contact with our Maker. While experiencing the intensity of the furnace of affliction, we look helplessly to the only One who can meet our needs. Even the hardest of hearts melt under such conditions. The prayers of unbelievers may be void of any biblical pattern. They may be rote prayers that are repeated over and over again in order to try to get God's attention. Perhaps they are prayers quoted out of some liturgical book, but although the prayers may not be biblical in form, they come from a heart that is hurting and trying to reach the only One who has the answer to a person's dilemma.

As believers in the Lord Jesus Christ, we have been informed concerning the Father's desire for fellowship with us. We are assured that He loves us, and our prayers to Him infuse confidence within us as we struggle to have faith in the great unseen reality who we worship. Prayer is not something that someone can teach you. Neither can you learn it from a book. Prayer is learned as it is exercised daily. It is learned by being still before God, waiting for His answer, believing without seeing, and trusting although you may have no indication of His answer. Oh, the delight of being in the presence of the all-sufficient One, the joy of knowing that we are sheltered in the tabernacle of His grace, to know that we are speaking to the One who has all the answers that we need—such an experience is a foretaste of heaven. It is an introduction to the kind of wonder and amazement that we will have as we enter the heavenly state and experience an overwhelming joy and complete satisfaction with no doubts and fears about anything.

Can you imagine how Moses must have felt as he spent forty days in the direct presence of God? When you consider the greatness of God, it is no wonder that Moses's face glowed as he came down off of the mountain. I have seen Christians who have a glow in their countenance that sets them apart from most who don't. They were not born with that smile on their face. What you see radiating from those people is the glow of the Spirit within. It is the manifestation of who God is and what He does in the lives of those who surrender to Him and walk with Him with a heart of integrity. Just the fact that God wants to be with us is indeed an incredible thing. And it is amazing when you consider the fact that although there are billions of people on this planet, God treats them all as individuals. He doesn't have a team of angels who help Him hear the prayers of seeking souls. God chooses to be as close to us as we are willing to be close to Him. How much of God do you want in your life? Are you satisfied with simply saying a few words to God each day? How important is fellowship with God to you compared to all of the other things in your life? And do you really want to hear His will for your life?

There are three kinds of listeners: First is the passive listener who doesn't want to hear from God at all. Then there is the selective listener who listens to only what he wants to hear. Then there is the aggressive listener who says with Samuel in the Temple, "Speak, Lord, for your servant is listening" (see 1 Samuel 3:10). It is that kind of submissive and open attitude that God showers His greatest blessings on.

Isaiah 50:4 says, "The Sovereign LORD has given me an instructed tongue, to know the word that sustains the weary. He wakens me morning by morning, wakens my ear to listen like one being taught." Can you imagine God saying to you every morning, "Good morning! Can I have a little time to talk with you? I have some great things I want to share with you before you get started on your day."

God is in the business of speaking to His people, and you can be someone who is so intimate with God that you obtain that heavenly glow. There are, however, a few things you will need. First, you need a designated time when you regularly meet with God. Intimacy with God is not at its highest level when you are weaving in and out of traffic. It is also important that you spend time with God in an environment where you will not be interrupted by noise. Several passages of Scripture emphasize the importance of solitude in our lives. Psalm 46:10 says, "Be still, and know that I am God." And Psalm 62:1 (NASB) says, "My soul waits in silence for God only; from Him is my salvation." In Lamentations 3:26-28, Jeremiah said, "It is good to wait quietly for the salvation of the LORD. It is good for a man to bear the yoke while he is young. Let him sit alone in silence, for the LORD has laid it on him." We also know that Jesus regularly retreated into solitude to pray and listen to the Father (see, for example, Mark1:35 and Luke 5:16).

Make a decision that you are going to become someone who doesn't just know about God, but someone who really knows God intimately. Doing so is the best decision you will ever make.

Oh, God, how much we need Your help every day. We are so easily distracted, and we honestly don't have the hunger for You that we need to have. Help us to seek You above all other things in our lives. This we pray in the name of our Lord and Savior, Jesus Christ. Amen.

CHAPTER 49

WHAT WE LEAST LIKE TO DO

When I was growing up, my mother would sometimes get the idea that I needed to eat turnip greens or brussels sprouts or something yucky like spinach. If it would have been left up to me, I would never have put that stuff in my mouth. I would have voted to make my vegetables cookies, ice cream, and candy. That way, Mom would have been happy, and I would have been happy.

It is interesting that some of the things that are on one person's "least liked" list may be on someone else's "most liked" list. For example, some people like snakes, and they keep them in their home in a terrarium as pets. Personally I am not a snake lover. I do not have any fondness in my heart for those reptilian creatures. I also don't like most of the entertainment at amusement parks. Let me sit and watch people perform, or show me some new technology, and I will be happy, but please do not ask me to ride on a roller coaster, a Ferris wheel, or any of those machines that take you up high and then plunge you down at lightning speed. Neither do I like the rides that whirl and turn you upside down, or that throw you from left to right. I know that when some people get off of those machines, they run as quickly as possible to get back in line so that they can do it again. Don't be surprised if you see me running the opposite direction. The point is that we all have a list of things that we would not want to do.

May I suggest one thing that none of us like doing? It is called "forgiveness." We do not naturally want to forgive. We would rather do something to hurt that person who has hurt us. We would rather have imaginary conversations raging in our minds as we mentally rehearse what we would like to say in reality. In our imaginary conversation, we are undefeatable. Our words are quick and to the point, and they pierce the heart of the one whom we are in conflict with. We are winning in our little mind game, and sometimes we rehearse that victory over and over again until our anger has intensified to the place that we have become thoroughly bitter and thoroughly miserable.

On the other hand, many times, the person with whom we are so upset has no idea about what is going on in our minds. They are having a good time while we stew, fret, and churn. In such situations, we need to listen to ourselves and then consider what God thinks about our thoughts. When God looks into an embittered heart, He sees sin and pollution.

If I remember correctly, the Lord Jesus had something to say to Peter about forgiveness (see Mathew 18:21-35), and there is no question about the fact that we are commanded to forgive. In fact, forgiveness is a Christian virtue. In contrast to the world's methods, God's way is forgiveness.

Consider these words from the heart of the apostle Paul. In Ephesians 4:32, it says, "Be kind and compassionate to one another, forgiving each other, just as in Christ God forgave you." Then, in Colossians 3:13, Paul says, "Bear with each other and forgive whatever grievances you may have against one another. Forgive as the Lord forgave you." And in 1 Corinthians 13:5, he says, "[love] keeps no record of wrongs." The Message translation says it this way: "[Love] doesn't keep score of the sins of others." Love doesn't keep score because love purposely has a bad memory. It finds a way to forget the sins of others. One of the reasons that it is difficult for us to forgive is the fact that we don't really understand what forgiveness is. We seem to think that forgiveness is forgetting what has been done. Forgiveness does not mean forgetting. It means that we choose to no longer hold of that sin against that person. We will not try to retaliate.

Instead we will choose to act toward that person as if he has never sinned against us. In the Old Testament on the Day of Atonement, the high priest would take two goats. He would slay one goat as he offered it as a sacrifice for the sins of the people, and he would send the other goat—the scapegoat—into the wilderness, and it would never come back. That scapegoat represented the fact that the sins which had been forgiven would never return. That is biblical forgiveness. It is choosing to not seek revenge. It is acting as though nothing negative has happened.

Sometimes we do things that we don't want to do, like eating turnip greens or spinach. I might even get on a roller coaster one day (but don't count on it). Whether we do those things or not makes very little difference. On the other hand, forgiveness will make all the difference in the world in our lives. It sets us free from a prison of our own making and allows joy and peace to return to what has been a heart consumed with poison and bitterness. Is there someone that you need to forgive? Is there someone who consumes much of your thought life because of what he has done to you? Life is too short to hold ourselves in bondage. We need to let go of the offenses that have been committed against us and know that we serve a God who can work all things together for our good (see Romans 8:28). Years after his brothers had sold him into slavery, Joseph said to them, "You intended to harm me, but God intended it for good to accomplish what is now being done, the saving of many lives" (Genesis 50:20).

We serve a God who is big enough to overrule the bad things people may do to us. Let's pour the poison out of our hearts and focus our attention on His goodness.

Father in heaven, You have forgiven us so much, and we are so unwilling to forgive the little that others have done against us. Please forgive us and help us to forgive those who sin against us as You have forgiven us when we have sinned against You.

CHAPTER 50

WAITING

Psalm 40:1-2 says, "I waited patiently for the LORD; he turned to me and heard my cry. He lifted me out of the slimy pit, out of the mud and mire; he set my feet on a rock and gave me a firm place to stand."

The art of waiting is not one that many of us possess. In fact, it is one of the least enjoyed activities imaginable. In our modern society, people generally have a lot of things on their plates, and it is common for us to travel at "warp speed" in our attempt to get everything done. You jog into the grocery store in hopes of quickly picking up a few items, only to find the store thoroughly congested with shoppers who are leisurely pushing their buggies as they carefully examine each product. When you look toward the checkout lines, you find every one of them filled beyond capacity. No matter where you go or what you do, it seems that you are called upon to exercise your "waiting" skills. If you get on the freeway, you find that it has become a parking lot, and you are sitting in the middle of it. Go to the doctor's office, and you will find the schedule to be running forty-five minutes behind. You need a job, and you are doing everything to get your résumé out to as many companies as possible, but you are not getting any response.

As difficult as those scenarios may seem to be, they are not the hardest kind of waiting. The hardest kind of waiting is waiting on God to answer a prayer that you have been asking about for months. You are diligently asking, but you have not seen even the slightest indication that God is listening. Each day that your prayers remain unanswered only brings more questions. Is there sin in your life that is keeping God from answering, or is your faith not strong enough? Are your motives wrong? Is God even there? The whole situation does not seem fair. You feel like saying with the psalmist in Psalm 42:9, "I say to God my Rock, 'Why have you forgotten me? Why must I go about mourning, oppressed by the enemy?'"

Yes, waiting is hard, but you are not the only one who has experienced the confusion of unanswered prayer. The Bible has a number of examples of godly people who had to wait on the Lord. God gave young Joseph prophetic dreams about his future position as a leader, but the fulfillment to that promise didn't come quickly. To the contrary, Joseph was thrust into some difficult places, including prison. Why would the God who promised a position of leadership to Joseph allow him to waste years sitting in an Egyptian prison? Ah, but those years were not wasted. They were spiritual character-building days, days through which Joseph learned to rely on God. The Lord knew that Joseph needed the experience of the prison before he could enjoy the experience of the palace. We must remember that God is a God of preparation.

We see it in David's life. When he was only a young man, Samuel anointed David to be the next king of Israel. He was God's chosen vessel, but he had to experience the furnace of affliction before he could become the greatest king Israel ever had. Abraham was another man who joined the fraternity of those who had to wait. God promised Abraham a son in his old age, and he believed what the Lord had promised. Like Joseph and David, Abraham had to learn to be what he needed to be before he could do what he needed to do, and that education came through waiting. Year after year passed, and still there was no promised son. Abraham even tried to help God by having a son through his servant girl, Hagar, but Abraham's plan was not God's plan. That meant Abraham had to continue waiting. For twenty-five years, Abraham waited for what must have seemed to be an impossibility, but with God, nothing is impossible. The day came when the promised son was born to Abraham's wife Sarah, and God fulfilled His promise.

The obvious question for Joseph, David, and Abraham—and for us—is "Why?" Why is it that God sometimes allows His faithful ones to go through such hard times? It is because they are faithful that God allows them to be trained to be even more faithful. What is accomplished in your life while you are waiting in prayer is often more important than the thing that you are asking for. While it was true that Abraham needed a son, it was also true that Abraham's son needed a father who had grown strong in faith over many years while waiting on God. Isaac could not have been what he was unless Abraham had become what he became.

Waiting on God is sometimes the only thing that can extract you from your self-centeredness and sin. The pressure of waiting causes you to become so desperate that you become willing to open up your tight fist and let God take what He wants out of your life. If God answered immediately, you would miss the growth that comes through the spiritual "muscle building" that comes from waiting. Your waiting is building in you a faith that will not waver and that will not quit. The faith that grows in your heart during your waiting brings great pleasure to the Almighty, and it becomes a witness to unbelievers who see within you a power that proves the reality of what you believe.

Psalm 42:5 says, "Why are you downcast, O my soul? Why so disturbed within me? Put your hope in God, for I will yet praise him, my Savior and my God." Amen and amen! Thank God for His wisdom and faithfulness!

> *Lord, help us to be willing to wait on You and Your plan for us.*
> *Give us patience as we wait on You. Amen.*

CHAPTER 51

LIVING IN UNCERTAIN TIMES

I don't think any of us would argue the point that we are living in uncertain times. Our economy is suffering, and many are in serious financial difficulties. It's not that there haven't been hard times before. My parents went through the Great Depression and World War II. I grew up in the turbulent '60s, and my generation was engaged in the Vietnam War. Since that time, there has been no shortage of unsettling events. Who among us will ever be able to forget 9/11 and the suffering and shock that accompanied that terrible event. We have witnessed the shedding of American blood in Iraq and other places, but its seems as though we have raised the anxiety level in these past few years. There is a growing threat of further terrorism in our country. If you are walking through the mall, you have no assurance that the man walking next to you doesn't have a bomb strapped around his chest. In addition, many nations are seeking to develop nuclear weapons—none of whom have any business doing so—and we know that once people start "punching buttons," our whole planet is going to be the loser. The real problem is stated in Psalm 11:3: "When the foundations are being destroyed, what can the righteous do?"

Even more, in Luke 6:48-49 (NLT), Jesus said:

"It is like a person building a house who digs deep and lays the foundation on solid rock. When the floodwaters rise and break against the house, it stands firm because it is well built. But anyone who hears and doesn't obey is like a person who builds a house without a foundation. When the floods sweep down against that house, it will collapse into a heap of ruins."

If the foundation of your house is bad, you are going to have real problems with your home. If the foundation of our nation is bad, we will have problems. If the foundation of your life is bad, you are going to have problems in your life. The most basic foundation is God Himself. To believe in a Creator God to whom we must one day give an account is the foundation of everything. If He did not exist, there would be no basis for absolutes and no reason for morality. But God does exist. His fingerprint has been stamped upon the world with all of its order and complexity. Not only does God exist, but we can be comforted by the fact that He is a faithful God. Many Scriptures testify of the faithfulness of God, including Deuteronomy 7:9, which says, "Know therefore that the LORD your God is God; he is the faithful God, keeping his covenant of love to a thousand generations of those who love him and keep his commands." And 1 Corinthians 1:9 says, "God, who has called you into fellowship with his Son Jesus Christ our Lord, is faithful."

Another fantastic passage that speaks of God's faithfulness is Joshua 21:43-45. It says:

So the LORD gave Israel all the land he had sworn to give their forefathers, and they took possession of it and settled there. The LORD gave them rest on every side, just as he had sworn to their forefathers. Not one of their enemies withstood them; the

LORD handed all their enemies over to them. Not one of all the LORD's good promises to the house of Israel failed; every one was fulfilled.

Simply put, Joshua said, "God did everything He told us He would do. He never failed, not even one time. God is faithful to us in the plans He has for us."

One of the favorite verses of many believers is found in Jeremiah 29:11. Speaking to the captives in Babylon, God said, "I know the plans I have for you . . . plans to prosper you and not to harm you, plans to give you hope and a future." Did you see that? God says he has a plan for His people, and that the plan is intended to do good for you. In the midst of billions of people living on this earth, God has you singled out, and He thinks about you. What a fantastic blessing!

How should we respond to such love? No matter how hard or threatening the circumstances might be, we should focus on God and keep moving in the direction He has chosen for us. "If God is for us, who can be against us?" (Romans 8:31). Trust in Him. Obey Him. Rejoice in Him, and you will find that at the end of the day, your life will be covered with His faithful blessings. He never fails.

Dear Lord, we come to You today in awe of Your wonderful love and faithfulness toward us. Help us, Lord, to remember Your faithfulness in our days of uncertainty.

CHAPTER 52

THE UNIVERSAL PURSUIT

As a child, one of the most frustrating things I experienced were those times when my mother decided that it was time for me to take a nap in the afternoon. It did no good to tell her that I was not tired and that I did not need a nap. Her mind was set, and I was destined to lie in the bed and look at the walls. I could try to entertain myself by looking at storybooks or by playing with a stuffed animal, but none of that could remove the frustration of being trapped in a bed that offered no satisfaction.

As I have grown older, I have often found that life is like lying in that bed during nap time. Whether you are lying in a bed during nap time as a child or lying in life's bed as an adult, you find yourself wanting something more. You become frustrated and long for the time to come when you can escape your present circumstances. The old saying is, "You make your bed and then you lie in it." The problem is that we are never satisfied with the bed that we are lying in. We are always in pursuit of something more, something different—that obscure thing that we have not yet discovered or have not yet achieved.

The book of Ecclesiastes tells the story of a frustrated man named Solomon who was not at all happy with the bed he was lying in. The book of Ecclesiastes is a record of how this man sought to change his circumstances and to find happiness apart from God. Solomon, who had been gifted by God with incredible wisdom, had fallen prey to the influences of pagan women and their pagan gods. As a result, he was led astray and no longer found God sufficient to meet his emotional needs. Ecclesiastes records the story of his pursuit of happiness. Unlike us, Solomon did not simply wish that he could have something. His incredible wealth allowed him to have anything he wanted. He tried it all, and he found it all to be insufficient. We can feel his frustration as he writes: "The words of the teacher, son of David, king in Jerusalem: 'Meaningless! Meaningless!' says the Teacher. 'Utterly meaningless! Everything is meaningless.'" He echoes the same discontent in Ecclesiastes 1:12-14 when he says:

I, the Preacher, was king of Israel in Jerusalem. I devoted myself to study and to explore by wisdom all that is done under heaven. What a heavy burden God has laid on men! I have seen all the things that are done under the sun; all of them are meaningless, a chasing after the wind.

The phrase "chasing the wind" says it all, because no matter how long you chase the wind, you will never catch it. Many things have changed since Solomon's time. We now live in a technological age that is advancing constantly. People no longer walk down dusty roads. They ride in cars, trains, or airplanes. If having things would make us happy, we should be the happiest generation that has ever lived, but as you look at the landscape of our society, you find that although many hundreds of years have passed, some things have remained the same. People are still chasing the wind in their pursuit of happiness, and none of them have ever caught the wind.

Everyone wants to be happy, but none know how apart from God. Some seek for recognition, some for fame, some for enjoyment, and others still for fortune, but they remain trapped and unsatisfied. I know this story well because I have been there and done that. Seeking happiness apart from God is like chasing after the wind. That is a universal truth that applies to all people in all circumstances all over the world.

Unless God is at the center of your life, nothing you do will ever be enough. On the other hand, having God and nothing else is enough. The apostle Paul, while confined to a dungeon, said,

> . . . I have learned to be content whatever the circumstances. I know what it is to be in need, and I know what it is to have plenty. I have learned the secret of being content in any and every situation, whether well fed or hungry, whether living in plenty or in want. I can do everything through him who gives me strength. (Philippians 4:11-13)

Clearly Paul had learned what Solomon was trying to discover when he wrote Ecclesiastes.

Life without God is like taking a nap that you don't want to take. The mattress may be soft, and the room may be beautiful, but it is not going to be enough. In contrast, enough is always enough when God is in control. In Colossians 2:10 (NASB), Paul wrote it this way: ". . . in Him you have been made complete . . . ." Completeness. What a blessed word! That means that you don't have to spend the rest of your life looking for something that will never be found. God reigning on the throne of your heart will give you inner freedom. Anything else is like trying to catch the air and put it in your pocket. God is waiting. It is your move.

Father in heaven, please forgive our misdirected attempts to find happiness apart from You. Help us to surrender our lives to Your will that You may fill us with the joy that You want Your children to have. Amen.

CHAPTER 53

THE ROLLER COASTER

Many years ago, my in-laws came to visit us when we were living in Florida. There were many things to do where we lived, but there was one thing that had to be done. Surely no one could visit Florida without also visiting the Magic Kingdom, so we pointed the car toward Orlando.

Entering Disney World is like being transported to a fairy-tale world with more than enough to keep you amazed for days. There are, however, a few things that are not for everyone. As we walked through the park, we came face-to-face with a giant structure that was an indoor roller coaster. The nearer we came to that instrument of torture, the more we were able to hear the screams of people. I had absolutely no desire to even get close to that machine, but I was under the impression that my mother-in-law wanted to ride it. So, trying to be a good son-in-law, I decided to ride it with her.

We got in line, and slowly but surely, we moved closer to what would be my greatest nightmare. As we advanced inside, we observed numbers of warning signs that cautioned people who had certain physical conditions to turn around and go back. Those signs were enough to make me run, but there was more. I had a clear view of those who exited the roller coaster. Some, barely able to stand, were leaning on others. It was obvious that they had just come through a traumatic experience, and I became more nervous by the moment. Finally the time I had most dreaded came. It was our turn to sit down and ride. In the midst of screaming thrill-seekers, we began moving faster and faster. We were jolted in one direction and then another. We went up and then shot downward at rocket speed. Feeling as though my heart was going to beat out of my chest, I did the only thing I knew to do. I tried to block the whole thing out of my mind and quoted Scripture. No one on the planet could have been any more grateful to get off of that roller coaster than I was, but it got worse. I found out that my mother-in-law did not really want to ride the roller coaster at all. She was only riding it to please me!

We are often like that roller coaster. Sometimes we are at the top, then something negative happens, and we find ourselves plunging down to the pit of despair. It does not help our Christian testimony to experience a "joy unspeakable and full of glory" (1 Peter 1:8 KJV) on Monday and then on Tuesday to reflect the words of Jeremiah the prophet: "For all these things I weep; tears flow down my cheeks" (Lamentations 1:16).

Why are we often up one day and down the next? How is it that we can say "praise the Lord" on one day and then act as though God does not exist the next day?

Could it be that we take God and His Word too lightly? All too often, we find ourselves not devoted to seeking God with our whole heart. We have not learned to enjoy time spent in His presence. We would rather watch TV than engage in an edifying Bible study. We would rather talk on the telephone to a friend than we would talk with our God. The result of that kind of negligent Christian living is that we are not filled with the Spirit. Instead we are filled with a knowing and growing sense of a need for something more.

That is when we begin to think about what we want that God has not given us rather than thinking about what He has given us. We find ourselves frustrated because we don't have more, when in reality, we have all that we need in Jesus Christ. We have also not believed the statement of Jesus that it is more blessed to give than that to receive (see Acts 20:35). We are blessed when we help someone who is in desperate need. We also experience overcoming joy when we share the Word of God and see someone growing spiritually due to our ministry. We are roller-coaster Christians because we're not filling our lives with God. As a result, we find ourselves often defeated. We need to learn that in the Christian life, it is selflessness rather than selfishness that brings consistent joy.

Father in heaven, help us to want to be with You, not because of what You can give us but because of who You are and who we may become.

CHAPTER 54

THE GREATEST THING IN LIFE

W hat is the greatest thing in life? Ask people that question, and you are sure to get a lot of different answers. The man who has not eaten in days will tell you the greatest thing in the world is some food to eat. Ask the man who has been diagnosed with cancer, and he will tell you the greatest thing in the world is to discover the diagnosis is incorrect. Ask the person who is stranded in a hot desert with no water, and he will answer, "Water." For a couple in love, the greatest thing in life may be to be married. If you had asked the question to Muhammad Ali when he was boxing, he would've answered, "I am the greatest!" The greatest thing in the world is not things or achievements. Relationships with family and friends are priceless, but that is still not the greatest thing.

The greatest thing possible is to have a relationship with the true and living God by spending time worshipping Him. Worship is the highest calling we have because it was for worship that we were created. Jesus said in John 4:23-24 that the Father seeks people to worship him "in spirit and in truth." Where does worship come from? Real worship happens when the Holy One ignites our hearts with the presence of His love, and we humbly stand in awe of our great God. Worship captivates our attention. It engages our minds, our emotions, and our will to the extent that God is our only focus. When Moses saw the burning bush in the desert, he was awestruck. It was enough that a bush would not extinguish itself, but when God spoke out of the bush, that was almost more than he could take. When God called Abraham, all Abraham's former dreams and passions were as if they had never existed. These men were totally captivated by God's presence. It is really difficult to describe the experience of worship because worship is not like anything else on earth, and it produces fulfillment, satisfaction, peace, and joy that nothing else can.

Worship is at the pinnacle of all mankind's experiences. It is the mountain peak of our existence. You may be an engineer, but your primary mission in life is worship. You may be a famous doctor, but your primary goal in life is to become a great worshipper. How then do we go about worshipping this great King? The first and foremost thing in worship is that we offer ourselves to God.

People throughout history have always worshipped God by the giving of a sacrifice. The first recorded sacrifices were from Cain and Able. We know that Noah offered sacrifices after the flood, and Abraham was asked to sacrifice his son. The Law, according to Moses, required sacrifices to be made for sin, and Jesus is described as our sacrificial lamb. Today, as you are one of God's spiritual priests, He wants you to offer not a lamb but a life—your life. Romans 12:1 says, "Therefore, I urge you, brothers, in view of God's mercy, to offer your bodies as living sacrifices, holy and pleasing to God—this is your spiritual act of worship." As we place our lives on the altar before God, we do so with a sincere humility. Psalm 95:6-7 says, "Come, let us bow down in worship, let us kneel before the LORD our Maker; for he is our God, and we are the people of his pasture, the flock under his care." Verse 7 says "for he is our God." What an incredible statement that is. He is not my fellow church member's God. He is not my pastor's God. He is my God! It is because He is my God that I should offer my body a living sacrifice as my spiritual act of worship. How can I do anything less? Worship is not only the greatest experience in life, it is the greatest transformational experience in life. When I come into the presence of the true and living God and worship him in spirit and in truth, there is something that happens within my heart that changes it from a hard rock to a pliable piece of putty.

When Moses worshipped the Lord on the mountain, being in the presence of God actually caused his face to glow. Being with Jesus causes you to become like Jesus. It makes you who you could never be otherwise. There is not only a sense of solemn humility in worship, there is also a supernaturally given joy that accompanies true worship. In Psalm 95:1-2, the psalmist said, "Come, let us sing for joy to the LORD; let us shout aloud to the Rock of our salvation." What is the greatest thing in life? The greatest thing in life is to be in harmony with God and to lavish upon Him all that I am or ever will be. It is a sense of radical abandonment of my selfish will in order to give myself to his will. Be careful that you don't trade the rags of this world for the royal robe of heavenly worship. Are you a true worshiper of God? When is the last time you truly offered yourself as a living sacrifice to God and experienced the joy that comes from that offering? The greatest thing in this life is to know and to worship the One who gave us life. Make it your goal to give God the glory that He deserves by your adoration of His Being.

Our Father in heaven, You are good, and You show Your love to us in so many ways. Please help us to learn to worship You. We pray this in Jesus's name. Amen.

CONCLUSION

L ife is filled with various circumstances, some of which we would consider to be good and others that we would consider to be bad. One thing is for sure: life is a journey, not a destination. Life is an ever-moving stream, always moving forward day after day, week after week, month after month, and year after year. It goes where it will, and no one can slow it down or stop its movement. Sometimes it takes us along familiar surroundings. At other times, it takes us places that we never thought we would be. It twists and turns, and no one can be absolutely sure where it will take us next.

Most of us do not take the journey alone. We share it with companions that travel with us, people like parents, children, spouses, and other significant figures. And then something strange happens. If we stay on the journey long enough, we find ourselves losing some of our fellow travelers. Their journey has ended while ours continues. Sometimes the journey seems too slow, and at other times, we can hardly keep up with the pace, but still we go on. The only constant thing that we can depend upon is God Himself. He was there with us when we started this journey, and He will be there when we end it.

It is my prayer that the chapters of this book have identified with some of your own life experiences and that they have given a biblical perspective on those experiences. I have given numbers of personal examples from my life, and each of you could offer your own stories as well. The truth is that we are all in this thing called "life" together, and we will all have our share in both the helpful and the hurtful, the times of great joy and the times of great sorrow. We know what it is to fly like an eagle, and we know what it is to sink like a rock. We have rejoiced at the birth of children, and we have waded through the waters of bereavement.

How then should we respond? First, we should be thankful for those who are traveling with us. Without them, the journey would certainly be much harder. Yes, we should be thankful for them, but what's more, we should find ways to show our appreciation. Second, we should realize that each day we have is a gift from God. If the journey continues today, we should live it as if it were the last, because it may be. Whether we have one year left or one day, we should seek to glorify God because without Him, there would be no journey at all.

He is the great Creator and Sustainer of all things. He is the Alpha and the Omega, the Beginning and the End, the First and Last. Unlike us, He knows no journey, for He is in the constant present tense. He alone knows the intricacies of our journey, and He alone can make it successful. To live without dependence upon Him is to guarantee failure. On the other hand, living in His will guarantees success, for success can be boiled down to two words: pleasing God.

If I am pleasing God in the journey of life, then it does not matter what others may think of my progress or lack thereof. I can be fulfilled in knowing that I am completing the reason for my existence. One day, it will be I who finishes the journey, and I will join the Lord in an existence filled with glory, joy, peace, and an absolute fulfillment that I can never know until that time. Until then, I must be faithful. So stay faithful, fellow traveler. Give God your best, and He will give His best to you.

CPSIA information can be obtained at www.ICGtesting.com
Printed in the USA
LVOW060505190413

329666LV00001B/4/P